**Start Programming with Visual Basic.NET**

**Start Programming with Visual Basic.NET**

**An Introduction to Visual Basic.NET**

# Table of Contents

# Projects

# Appendix

## Register Your Copy

If you email me your comments, suggestions, or changes on the book or even to point our mistakes in the book, or to just say, "Hey, I bought your book.", as I develop material I will forward it to you. Lesson Plans, Projects, additional chapters, quiz questions, videos, are all in the various stages of development. Help me keep your book current and useful in the classroom.

I promise I will not sell or give your email address or distribute it, or sell it. It will only be used for me to contact you about new material.

My email address is: jkelley742@gmail.com

My web site is: http://www.gurus4pcs.com

# INTRODUCTION

For years, I have been teaching a course that introduces Visual Basic.NET programming. I decided to put my notes on paper in a form that would serve as a text for the lessons of the course, in the order and the way I teach.

I have had success with my approach and I hope all who use this in their classes or for their own self study, find it worthwhile.

As a user and proponent of Open Source Software, this book was written in its entirety using Apache OpenOffice.org. I used the Apache OpenOffice Writer to convert it to a PDF for distribution. The screenshots were created using either Paint.NET or GIMP, both free softwares available for download from their internet sites.

The only commercial software required for this course is Visual Basic. I used Visual Studio 2010 and 2013 to create the examples. If the cost of purchasing Visual Basic or Visual Studio is a problem, Microsoft makes an Express Edition of Visual Basic that can be downloaded from their web site at NO cost. All examples and exercises can be done using Visual Basic Express.

# FOR THE INSTRUCTOR:

One of the most frustrating parts of teaching computer related subjects is the books. There are many good books on many subjects. However, I find that for some courses I don't need 24 chapters on a topic that force my instruction into that chapter pattern or sequence. Often I would like a few chapters or even sections from a book, arranged in my sequence, and supplemented by my notes to create a lesson or part of a course.

VB textbooks available are many and varied, for the most part quite good. But, I just needed a few basic lessons to allow me to introduce Computer Studies majors to the basic concepts of VB programming at the beginner level. Also, I am fighting the tendency to teach the way I learned, with long laborious lectures on theory. I find that today's student suffers from what I call "The Sesame Street Syndrome". That is learning in 5 to 10 minute segments in an entertaining way. So, now we must adjust to the new paradigm of teaching and learning. I began this work in an attempt to match this learning pattern. Small segments of lessons with lots of hands on activities.

## FOR THE STUDENT:

I divided the subject matter into small lessons.  Each lesson topic has a short explanation and most have an example of how to use the code or a Step-by-Step exercise to demonstrate the use of the concept studied.  Programming is learned by hands-on not by reading about it.  Do the exercises, make the mistakes, find the mistakes and learn from them.  It takes years to produce a real programmer, so be patient and practice your skills repeatedly.

## SUPPLEMENTS:

It is my intention to supplement this book with a web page.  This way I can provide updates to the material on a moments notice.  We are teaching in a field where change is good, frequent and where printed copy does not stand the test of time. Test banks while nice, often leave the instructor explaining why a question was wrong.  Sometimes I have found that I agree with the student and have no rationale as to why the test bank had a different answer.  So, don't expect big fancy test banks.  Perhaps some questions that I use in my classes but in a format the instructor can modify to their own satisfaction.  Programming Exercises as I come up with new material would be included in a supplemental web page.  Once again, use what you like or make your own.  PowerPoint slides are not part of my teaching method.  I find they lead to dull lectures where the students snooze and print out the slides later and feel they are getting everything the lecture had to offer.  Better yet, use CamStudio or Jing (for free) to create a short video lesson.  Use YouTube and make a movie and post it to make your point in an interesting format.  Although videos are simply short lectures, they are more popular than sitting in class and if you keep them short and to the point they will be used.  The great part is that they can be repeated by the student until they understand the concept.

## SUMMARY

I am a computer programmer who turned teacher.  I see a need in my own classroom  for a text with lots of examples that take a student through creating Visual Basic programs, step by step.  Hands on is the way to learn programming and this text is designed to facilitate the students hands on experience.  This text gives the theory in text for reference or reading, then examples written to lead a student through practicing the theory with step by step examples.  So,  here is my attempt to teach Visual Basic Programming, Step-by-Step.

# UNIT 1

Lesson 1: Microsoft Visual Basic.NET Overview

Lesson 2: Creating Forms

Lesson 3: Event Driven Programming

# Lesson 1
## Microsoft Visual Basic.NET an Overview

### 1.1 Overview of Microsoft Visual Basic.NET

Visual Basic.NET 2012 is part of Visual Studio 2013. It is an environment for the development of computer programs. The Visual Basic.NET programming environment combines a graphical interface and programming code to make a Rapid Development Programming Environment.

Visual Studio is an IDE (Interactive Development Environment) containing the tools to create, debug, test, and run VB.NET programs.

Visual Studio and Visual Basic.NET are Microsoft products that must be purchased and installed on your computer before you can attempt any of the exercises in this book.

Once installed, starting VB.NET is a simple process. However, the process may vary depending on the version purchased and the install options used to install Visual Studio or Visual Basic.NET.

#### 1.1.1 Step by Step Exercise
1. Click on the Start Button
2. Select All Programs (or Programs) menu.
3. Find and Select Visual Studio (if installed)
4. Find and Select Visual Basic.NET
5. The start page for Visual Studio (or Visual Basic) should appear.

### 1.2 Using an Existing Project

Visual Basic stores files in a project folder. A project may contain several programs. The main project file has an extension of *.vbproj* where project information is stored.

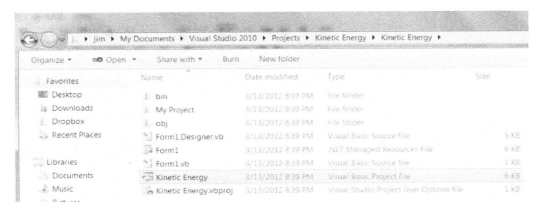

**Figure 1.2.1**

There is a solution file with an extension of *.sln* that is a composite of all projects store within the folder. We will only be concerned with single project solutions in this book. However, we will open existing programs using the .sln file. While it is possible to open with the .vbproj file, it is highly recommended that you get in the habit of using the .sln file.

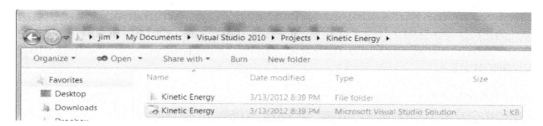

*Figure 1.2.2*

A common mistake many beginners make is to only save the .sln file to an external drive and expect to open the project from just that file. It is important that you save the ENTIRE project file to transfer your work to an external drive.

Another way to open an existing project is to select it from the Start page of Visual Studio or Visual Basic. They are listed under "Recent Projects". It lists the most recent projects compiled in the current system and exist in the default folder for VB projects. (Project folders exist in Users > MyDocuments > Visual Studio 20xx > Projects)

If you don't see the project you wish to open, click on the "Open Project" selection and navigate to the folder containing your project.

*Figure 1.2.3*

Note, Visual Basic may not open the Form on loading. To correct this, go to the Solution Explorer and double click on the form name you wish to open.

## 1.2.1 Step by Step Exercise

Open a New Project and Name it MyFirstProgram. (See Figure 1.2.2.1)

#1 Make Sure Visual Basic is selected in Recent Templates
#2 Select "Windows Form Application".
#3 Name the Project "MyFirstProgram".
#4 Click on OK

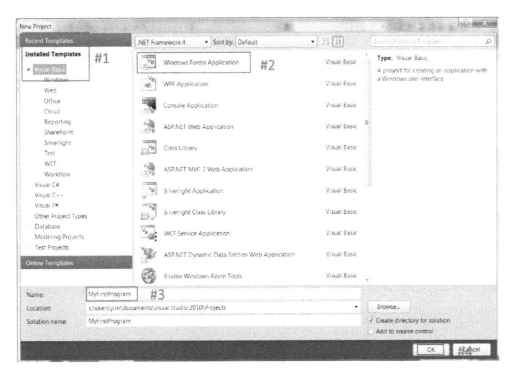

*Figure 1.2.2.1*

It is important to insure the Visual Basic template is selected when using Visual Studio. It is a common mistake to jump right to the Name and click on OK before reviewing all of the parameters on the dialog box. This may look ok at this point but can come back to cause problems in a later step.

In the lower right corner of the dialog box there is a checkbox that is titled "Create directory for solution", it is also a good idea to make sure this box is checked.

When you type a name in the Name text box it is repeated int the textbox that is titled "Solution Name:". Both text boxes should contain the same name. This applies to all programs we will be writing in this course.

Then, when you click on the OK button you will see the IDE and it will look similar to the example in Figure 1.2.2.2.

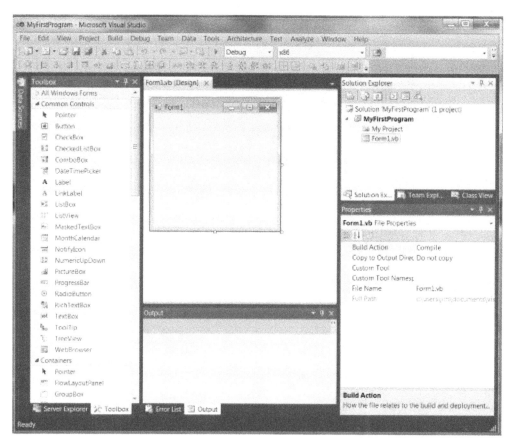

**Figure 1.2.2.2**

Visual basic has now created a working program. Yes, this program may now be excuted and will compile to an .exe file if you did everything exactly as outlined.

To compile this program go to the menu across the top and look for a menu selection named "Debug". (See Figure 1.2.2.3)

**Figure 1.2.2.3**

Clicking on the Debug menu item will result in a dropdown menu.

Select the item "Start Debugging    F5". The F5 is a shortcut. If you just hit the F5 key it is the same as selecting Debug → StartDebugging. Either way, the new application will be executed and result in a new window as shown in Figure 1.2.2.4.

**Figure 1.2.2.4**

To close the program go to the top menu and the leftmost selection is "File". Click on File and a dropdown menu appears. The very last item in this sub menu is "Exit". Select Exit and the program will end. (See Figure 1.2.2.5)

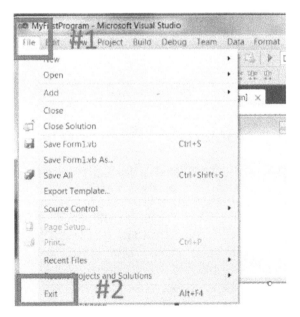

**Figure 1.2.2.5**

15

Now we have a new application stored on our hard drive.  Now we want to move this to our Flash Drive so we can work on this program on a different computer.

In the example below (Figure 1.2.2.6) I signed on to the computer as Username: jim.  The default location for storing our Visual Basic Projects is under the MyDocuments folder.  In the MyDocuments folder you will find a sub folder named "Visual Studio 2010" (or a similar name for other versions – Express users may See Visual Basic Express 20xx).

One of the subfolders in this folder is titled "Projects".  Under Projects you will see a list of folders as you named them when creating the projects.  Look for the folder named "MyFirstProject".

This is the folder you want to copy, in its entirety, to your flash drive.  Remember you need ALL of the files in this folder to replicate your project on another computer.

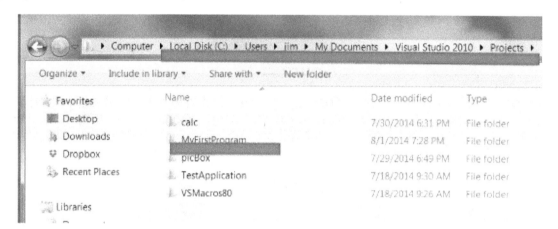

*Figure 1.2.2.6*

## 1.3   Compiling a Project

When you successfully compile a Visual Basic program, an executable file is produced.  This file has a .exe extension.  This file can be run on any Windows computer that has the .NET framework installed.  To create an executable file that runs on other Windows operating systems without the .NET framework, is possible but will not be discussed in this course.  The .NET framework is a free download from the Microsoft web site.

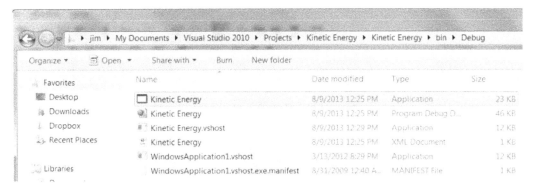

*Figure 1.3.1*

### *1.3.1 Step by Step Exercise*

To find the application in the Projects folder (Find the .exe file) you need to look in the following subfolder.

**Projects**
   [project name] – A subfolder under Folder Projects
      **bin** – A subfolder in the selected project folder
         **Debug** – A subfolder in the bin folder.

In the Debug folder you will find the .exe file. This file can be saved, and transported to another computer and run as an application.

## *1.4   Running a Visual Basic Program*

When a program has been successfully compiled, the program can be run from the IDE. You will use this method to test your programs. There are several ways to run the program and we will look at running the program from the IDE. Noting that there are several ways to run from the IDE. The simplest way is to press the F5 key at the top of the keyboard. A second way is to find the Debug menu, click on it and select "Start Debugging". A third way is to look for an icon with a green right arrow in the icon bar and click on it.

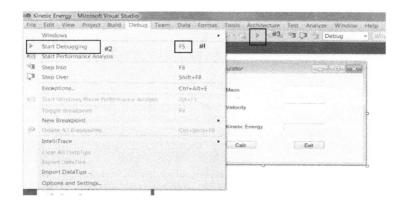

**Figure 1.4.1**

This results in running the current project, if there are no syntax or logic errors.  Any errors, all bets are off.


## 1.5   Exiting Visual Basic

To leave the Visual Studio or Visual Basic IDE, you can just select the File menu and then select Exit.  This is the recommended way to exit Visual Basic.  It is important to note that each time you compile your program, the new and changed files are saved.

## 1.6   Summary

Microsoft Visual Basic.NET is a component of Microsoft Visual Studio. You may experience it as part of Visual Studio, as a standalone product or as a Free Download known as Visual Basic Express.  All of these products support the programming addressed in these lessons.
Using the Microsoft Visual Basic.NET IDE (Interactive Development Environment), is the objective of this lesson.  It is important to be familiar with the elements of the IDE before beginning to learning how to program applications.
Starting existing projects as well as new projects is a great starting place.  This procedure will become automatic with enough practice.
Saving your project and moving it to another computer is another important concept.  Too often beginner programmers try to move selected files and this results in the loss of valuable work.  This lesson stressed the importance of moving the entire project folder.
Once there is a working application, the programmer can then find the compiled .exe file and move it to any computer that runs the Windows Operating system with the .NET framework installed.

**Lesson 2**
**Creating Forms**

## 2.1 *Creating a new Visual Basic Program*

Microsoft's Visual Studio allows for creating programs in several different languages. So, if you are using Visual Studio, it is important to insure you are working in the correct programming language each time you begin a new project.

The easist way to begin a new project is to select "New Project" on the Start screen.

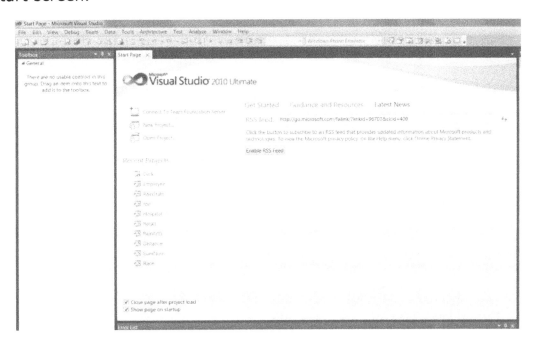

**Figure 2.1.1**

## 2.2 *The Visual Basic IDE*

Now that we have started the Visual Basic IDE, we need to look at the screen and understand the various parts of the Microsoft IDE.

1. Menu Bar
2. Toolbar
3. Solution Explorer
4. Properties
5. Toolbox
6. Design Box

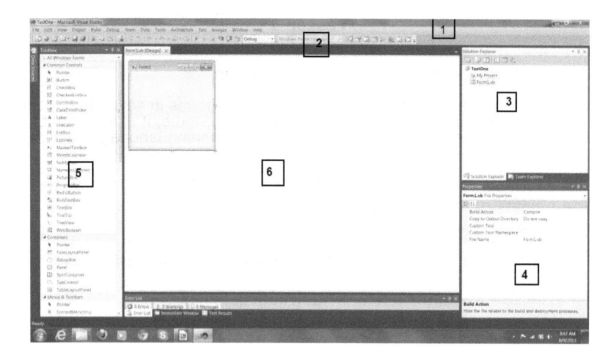

The **Menu Bar (1)** is the Microsoft standard menu format.  Click on a selection and there will be a drop down menu with items related.  The **Tool Bar (2)** is the bar where Icons represent many of the popular selections from the drop down menus.

The **Solution Explorer (3)** is the area that lists some of the files that make up the project.  This is where you can select files and modify some of the file properties, add new files and delete unwanted files.

The **Properties (4)** area is where properties for the selected object are shown.  This area is used to make changes to properties.

The **Toolbox (5)** is where the programmer can get controls to populate the form.  There are several areas of tools but this course will deal mostly with the Common Controls.

The **Design Area (6)** is where the form is designed, in design view and when code is required, and in code view this is where code will be written.

### 2.3  Saving a Project

As I noted in Lesson 1, all files are automatically saved when the program is compiled.  Another way to save is to click on File and then Save All.

It is important to make sure your work is saved before trying to copy the project folder or to start a new project.  The IDE when closed will remind you to save your work.  It is always a good idea to save your work often as you work through a program.  Each time you reach a point where you have significant work to protect, save it!

## 2.4   Form Properties

In object oriented terms, all objects (and the window created is an object) have properties.  Properties are used to describe the object. Things like color, size, title, location, are just a couple of the properties that VB uses to create instances of an object.  Click on the center area of the form and look at the projects window.   Note all of the different properties of the window (form) object.

### 2.4.1 Step by StepExercise

Open a new project and name it FormProperties
When the Form is generated, select the form so it has focus.
Examine the Form Properties.
Find the (Name) property
Change to "frmMain"
Find the Text Property
Change to "Main Form"
Find the BackColor Property
Select a background color
Find the Font Property
Change to Arial, Normal, 12
Find the ForeColor Property
Select a color for the text on the form.
Find the Size Property
Use the sizing handles on the form to change the size watch the value in the property change.

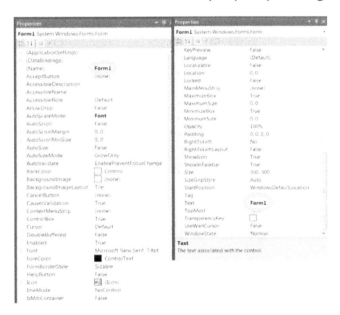

**Figure 2.4.1**

21

There are two form properties that we should always modify on creation, (Name) and Text.  Examine Figure 2.4.1 and find these properties.

## 2.5  Creating Controls

Controls are objects that are placed on the form (window).  Controls are taken from the toolbox and placed on the form.  The first controls we will work with are found in the Common Controls section of the Toolbox.

You can place a control on the form in two different ways.  First, you can double click on the control and it will be placed on the form.  It will be placed in the upper left corner or at the position of the last control placed on the form.  The second way is to single click on the control, the cursor turns to a + and then you can "draw" the control on the form.

**Figure 2.5.1**

Now, create a new form to practice the placement of controls on the form, naming the controls and changing other control properties.

### 2.5.1 Step by Step Exercise

**Create a new project**, name the project MyName.  Change the Form1 *name* property to *frmName*.  See Figure X.X.

22

**Create a label** for the heading and a second label for the output.  Do not change the name property of the first label, change its *text* property to *"My Name is"*  Change the *name* property of the second label to *lblMessage*.  Your form should look like the form in Figure X.X.

**Create a textbox** and place it as shown in Figure X.X.  Change the textbox *name* property to *txtName*.

**Create two buttons** on the form and place as shown in Figure X.X.  Name the first button *btnGo* and the *text* property to **GO**.  Name the second button *btnExit* and change the *text* property to **EXIT.**

Once the controls are placed on the form they can be moved, resized and even deleted using the method of clicking on the control and pressing the delete key on the keyboard.

To move a control you must first give it *focus*.  This means the control must be selected.  You select a control by single clicking on the control.  You can recoginze the selected control by the appearance of small boxes in the corners and midpoints of the sides.  (See Figure 2.5.2)  When the cursor is placed over a selected control, the cursor turns to a four sided arrow.

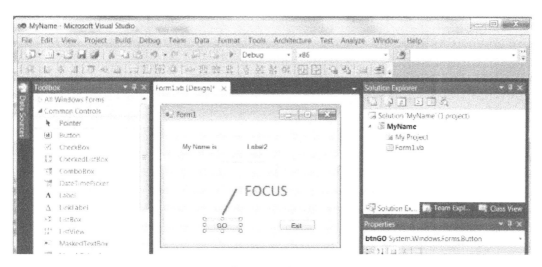

*Figure 2.5.2*

As the control moves, *snap lines*, appear to show you how the moving control lines up with other controls.  Blue lines show how the control lines up with other controls.  Red lines show how the text lines up with text in other controls.  (See Figure 2.5.3)

Move the controls around and experiment with the snap lines. When a form contains many different controls, the ability to use snap lines will help produce forms that are readable and look good.

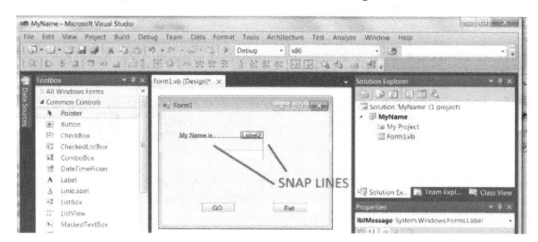

**Figure 2.5.3**

These are just some of the numerous aids provided by the Visual Studio/Visual Basic IDE. As you become familiar with the IDE you will discover other ways it has been designed to assist the designer in developing functional, attractive, and user friendly tools.

## 2.6   Changing Control Properties

Since a form is also an object, it has properties. The control's properties describe the control. When the control has focus, the properties section lists the controls properties. You can change the properties here. Some, but not all properties may also be changed at run time by code. We will only be looking at a few of the properties in this course. Many controls have identical properties.

**Figure 2.6.1**

24

Drop Down Arrow shows choices available for this property.

*Figure 2.6.2*

The elipsis (three dots) indicates that this property has an associated dialog box which is to be used to indicate the parameters for that property.  (See Figure 2.6.2)

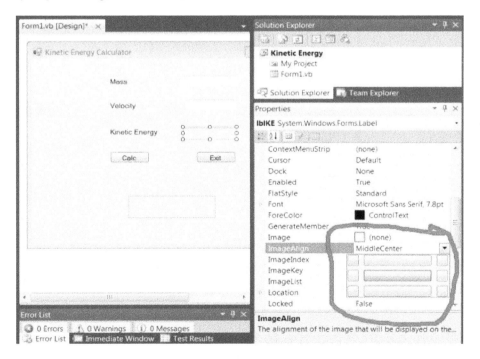

*Figure 2.6.3*

Another means of setting properties is the example as shown in Figure 2.6.3.  The figure shows a choice of positioning  an image within a control by clicking on the position in the control that is desired.

The control offers 9 different selections.  Selection is made by clicking on the desired location:

| | | |
|---|---|---|
| *Top Left* | *Top Center* | *Top Right* |
| *Middle Left* | *Middle Center* | *Middle Right* |
| *Bottom Left* | *Bottom Center* | *Bottom Right* |

The programmer has been directed to display the name in a 12 point, bold, script font.  The property to do this is the "Font" property.  The Font property is followed by an elipsis so, there is an associated dialog box.  As you do the exercise, examine the dialog box and the selections carefully.  (See Figure 2.6.4)  Understanding the options will be useful in further development efforts.  If you want to change the color of the font, the property below Font is ForeColor.  The font color is picked by selecting the color from a color picker dialog box.

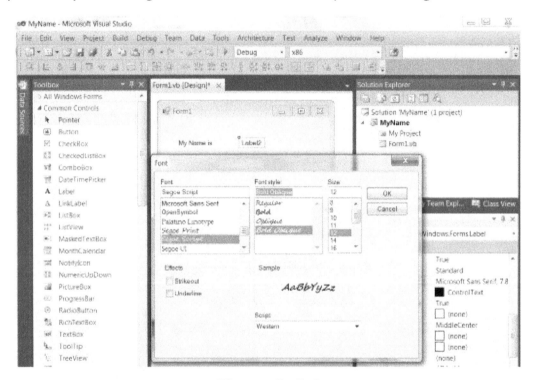

**Figure 2.6.4**

Note that when you select the font, style and size, the Sample shows what this font will look like on your form.

26

## 2.7  Summary

In this lesson we continued to explore the IDE (Interactive Development Environment).  The components like Menu Bar, Toolbar, Solution Explorer, Properties, Toolbox, and Design Box are identified and the programmer should be able to quickly identify the location, purpose and contents.

Properties of the objects are another important component of form design.  Where to find various properties and the effect of changing these properties.

Populating the form with controls is another key component of Visual Basic programming.  Each control has a specific purpose.  The controls we used in this lesson are: Label, TextBox, PictureBox, and Button.

Other important concepts in this lesson were: focus, snap lines, elipsis, dialog box, and properties.

# Lesson 3
# Event Driven Programming

## 3.1   Events

Event-driven programming is a term used to define a programming paradigm where the flow of the program is determined by events. Events are simply a change in data, a button click, a mouse click, a key press, a form loading, and literally hundreds of other signals produced by a program executing in memory.  Events may occur from a user action or something that happens during the execution of some code or something happens in the system.  These events always occur but only when the programmer writes code to be executed at that point, does it execute anything.

## 3.2   The Code Window

The "Code Window" is the area where you will enter your code for the various events you need to program.  There are several ways to enter this window.

First, go to the menu bar and click on View and then Code.

Second, double click on any part of the form or on any control.  This will also generate a click event for that control or in the case of clicking on the form it will generate a load event.

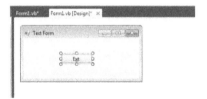

### Figure 3.2.1

Third, if the code window has already been opened for the project, there is a tab on the tab bar that may be clicked.

Fourth, go to the Solution Explorer and find the window that you are writing code for and right click on the formname.vb and select "View Code" from the drop down menu.

### Figure 3.2.2

Once in the code window you can select the control and event you wish to program and that will generate the Subroutine header and footer for that event.

## 3.3   Code Button Click Events

One of the more common control events is when the user clicks on a button to cause some action like a calculation or clearing the form or even to exit the form or the program.  These are called button click events.

### *Figure 3.3.1*

In Figure 3.3.1 we see a code window showing the Click event for a button named btnExit.  The first line "`Public Class Form1`" shows the start of the code for all events.  It is paired with the last line of the code window "`End Class`", this is the end of the area containing all events associated with Form1.  No code should be after this line and there is no reason for changing or deleting either the first line or the last line.  Doing so will cause errors in the program.

The line that begins with "`Private Sub btnExit....`" is the first line of the event.  This is called the subroutine header.  The line "`End Sub`" is the last line of the event and is referred to as the subroutine footer.  This event is tied to the click event of a button named btnExit.  The code for this event is found between the two lines.  In this case the code line is `Me.Close()` which is the statement used to close a form.

The subroutine header and footer are the container for the code to be executed when this event is triggered.  The code in the event will execute and when finished, the program may continue on to wait for another event or exit if that is what the last command executed in the event told the program to do.  Note: This code should NEVER be changed or deleted.

If the program or form does not exit, the program will then listen for the next event to be triggered.

To add the button control to your form, find the toolbox and identify the control named "Button".  Double click on this control and it will place the button control on your form.  You may then move the control to its proper place on the form.

Once the control has been placed on the form you should change the name property to properly name the control and the text property so its function is properly identified to the user.

### 3.3.1 Step-by-Step Exercise

Create a new Visual Basic project, name the project **picBox.**
Add a button control named *btnShow* with the text property "Show".
Add a second button control named *btnHide* with the text property "Hide".
Add a third button control named *btnExit* with the text property "Exit".
Add a fourth button control named btnStart with the text property "Start".
Place these controls as shown in Figure 3.3.2.

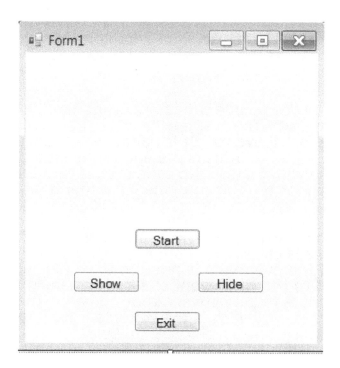

*Figure 3.3.2*

Now double click on the Exit button to get the code window with the click event for btnExit. Enter the code to close the form as shown in Figure 3.3.3.

*Figure 3.3.3*

Save your work but keep Visual Basic open for the next step by step exercise.

## 3.4   The Picture Control

Next we enter a Picture Box control.  The picture box control will hold an image and display it on the form.  The name of the picture will be in the Image property of the picture box control.  When we name the control the first three letters of the name should be pic followed by some discriptive name.  Example:  picMountains.

### 3.4.1 Step-by-Step Exercise

Place a picure box on our form, name it picCabin and follow these steps to get the picture on your form.

1. Make sure you have the picture named cabin.jpg on your desktop.
2. Give focus to the control named picCabin.
3. Find the property named Image and select.
4. A dialog box should appear.  Do the following in the dialog box:
    1. Click on the Radio Button "Local Resource:"
    2. Click on "Import" Button
    3. Navigate to the picture "cabin.jpg" on your desktop.
    4. Select the picture.
    5. Click on "Open" button.
5. Next steps require the control "picCabin" to have focus.
    1. Find the SizeMode property and change to StretchImage.
6. Your example should now look like Figure 3.4.1.1.
7. Save your work and keep open for the next exercise.

*Figure 3.4.1.1*

## 3.5   The Visible Property

Some times it is necessary to temporarily hide a control from the viewer.  This may be done to reduce "clutter" in the form or perhaps just show the control when necessary, for example, directions or an error message, etc..

Most controls have a visible property which may be set to either true or false.  Think about it, it is either visible or it is not visible.  Only two possible settings.

This control may be set to either true or false in the code or at design time, or both.

### 3.5.1 Step-by-Step Exercise

Give Focus to the "picCabin" control and change the Visible property to False.

Save your work and keep open for the next exercise.

## 3.6   The Enabled Property

Often a program disables controls until events take place that will cause the control to be enabled.  Perhaps the calculate button should not be enabled until all the necessary information has been entered.

In our program, this would be best illustrated by the Show button and the Hide button.  If the picture is visible, the Show button has no purpose so it should be disabled so as to not confuse the user.  Once the picture is made invisible, the Show button should be enabled and the Hide button disabled.

We will use the enabled property more extensively when we get into menus in a later lesson.

### 3.6.1 Step-by-Step Exercise

Give Focus to the "Show" button and change the Enabled property to False.

Give Focus to the "Hide" button and change the Enabled property to False.

Save your work and keep open for the next exercise.

## 3.7 *Using Code to Change Properties*

Many properties can be changed by code. NOT ALL properties may be changed by code, but many are changeable and programs made more flexible and useful by changing properties.

We have looked at the Name property. This is one that may NOT be changed as the program runs. The text property, the visible property and the enabled properties we examined in prior lessons are all changeable properties.

### 3.7.1 Step-by-Step Exercise

Now we will code the application. The code will involve changing various properties as the application runs and the user makes choices.

The code required is shown in Figure 3.7.1.1. In the design window give the SHOW button focus and double click to generate a click event for that button. Enter the code for the btnShow Click event as shown in Figure 3.7.1.1. Only the three lines of code between the Subroutine header and footer.

Return to the design view and double click on the Hide button to generate a click event for that button. Enter the code for the btnHide Click event as shown in Figure 3.7.1.1. Only the three lines of code between the Subroutine header and footer.

Return to the design view and double click on the Start button to generate a click event for that button. Enter the code for the btnStart Click event as shown in Figure 3.7.1.1. Only the four lines of code between the Subroutine header and footer.

Return to the design view and double click on the Exit button to generate a click event for that button. Enter the code for the btnExit Click event as shown in Figure 3.7.1.1. Only the one line of code between the Subroutine header and footer.

```
Public Class Form1

    Private Sub btnShow_Click(ByVal sender As System.Object, ByVal e As System.EventArgs) Handles btnShow.Click
        picCabin.Visible = True
        btnShow.Enabled = False
        btnHide.Enabled = True
    End Sub

    Private Sub btnHide_Click(ByVal sender As System.Object, ByVal e As System.EventArgs) Handles btnHide.Click
        picCabin.Visible = False
        btnShow.Enabled = True
        btnHide.Enabled = False
    End Sub

    Private Sub btnStart_Click(ByVal sender As System.Object, ByVal e As System.EventArgs) Handles btnStart.Click
        picCabin.Visible = False
        btnShow.Enabled = True
        btnHide.Enabled = False
        btnStart.Enabled = False
    End Sub

    Private Sub btnExit_Click(ByVal sender As System.Object, ByVal e As System.EventArgs) Handles btnExit.Click
        Me.Close()
    End Sub
End Class
```

***Figure 3.7.1.1***

Your code window should look EXACTLY like the contents of Figure 3.7.1.1.

If you have any red squggly or blue squggly underlines in the code window, you have an error. Start with spelling, a common mistake.

```
Private Sub btnShow_Click(ByVal sender As System.Object, ByVal e As System.EventArgs) Handles btnShow.Click
    picCabin.Vsible = True          #1
    btnShow.Enabled = False
    btnHide.Enabled = Tru           #2
End Sub
```

***Figure 3.7.1.2***

In Figure 3.7.1.2 the line titled #1 shows a blue squggly line. The error here is the property "Visible" is spelled incorrectly.

The line titled #2 shows a red underline. The parameter for Enabled property is incorrect. It can only be True or False.

Now, let us look at some other properties that may be changed by code. First the "Background" property for the form control. The background color is the color of the area of the control. For the form it is the entire form, for a button it is the color of the button, for a label it is the color of the label area, for a text box the color of the box, and so on for all controls with a background property.

Next, the Foreground property of a label control is the color for the text in a label control.  Change the foreground color to red and the text in the label will be red.

For those controls with a text property, this is the text displayed by that control.  The word(s) on a button, the message in a label, the title of a form are all examples of how the text property is displayed.

## 3.8   Access Keys

In some applications, one of the letters on the button or menu item is underlined.  This indicates that this is an **Access Key**.  An access key is usually a letter that when the Alt key is pressed in combination with that letter, it is the same as clicking on the button or menu item.  This allows those high speed data entry people to keep their hands on the keyboard.  Many consider it a waste of time to move a hand to the mouse button.  When you are paid for production, this can be a concern.

The access key is declared in the text property of the button control.  To make the 'x' key the access key for the Exit button simply put a '&' before the x, the text will look like:  E&xit.  Then when the Alt key is pressed at the same time as the x key is pressed, the click event for the Exit button will be executed.

## 3.9   AcceptButton and CancelButton Form Properties

The AcceptButton and the CancelButton are additional ways to keep those fingers on the keyboard.  These are both form properties and the form must have focus to view these properties.

The AcceptButton holds the command that will be executed when the Enter key is pressed.  The CancelButton holds the command that will be executed when the ESC key is pressed.

Normally the Enter key will select the OK button on a Message Box or Input Box.  The ESC key will select the cancel button on a Message Box or Input Box.

The AcceptButton property names the command button to be used when the enter key is pressed.  The CancelButton holds the name of the command button on the form that will be activated when the user presses the ESC key.

Remember, only ONE command button on a form can be attached to these properties.

## 3.10 Summary

This lesson brought you through setting up and coding an entire application.  Attention to detail is critical to successful programming.  A misplaced or misspelled word is a killer.  Not naming something correctly or not naming the control can lead to problems when coding.

Some properties can be changed with code, others only at design time.  Some properties change the look, others change how the user interface works.  Changing a property in the code is common in Visual Basic Programming.  Just think of those items on forms you have used that are not enabled until you perform some operation.  Or, think of buttons or information that pop up when you perform a certain action on a form.  You should now understand the basics and the reasons behind these operations.

# Unit Two – Working With Data

Lesson 4 – Variables

Lesson 5 – Calculations

Lesson 6 - Strings, Decimals and Objects

# Lesson 4
## Variables

### *4.1 Define Variables*

As a program runs it needs a place to store the data it is working with. The program cannot directly process numbers that were entered into text boxes or input boxes so it needs to convert the strings entered into numbers and often store them in the program for later processing.

The program creates storage spaces for data called variables. A variable is a named area of memory allocated to store a number, a string, an object, a character, and several other types of data commonly used by a program.

Since the computer only understands numbers and assigns a numeric address to each storage area, Visual Basic allows the programmer to assign names to these storage areas and specify what type of data that area should hold. The names help the programmer remember what data is stored in the space and the specified type allows VB to insure the correct type of data is stored in the storage space.

| Computer Address | User Assigned Address |
|---|---|
| 100203045 | decGrossPay |
| 100203053 | decPayRate |
| 100203061 | intHoursWorked |
| 100203065 | strEmployeeName |

The table does not represent actual addresses or memory locations it is only to illustrate the computer generated address is also given a programmer assigned address for programming purposes.

### *4.2 Data Types*

Since the computer only understands zeros and ones, everything is stored in the computer in numbers. When we declare storage places to store data, it is important to tell the computer what type of data will be stored in those places so it can interpret those numbers correctly. The computer will process the numbers in a String variable differently than it would process the numbers in a Decimal variable.

Declaring a data type helps the compiler reserve the correct number of memory locations to store that data that will be stored at that location.

This table shows the various data types, the number of bytes they occupy and the range of values that can be stored in that data type.

| Data Type | Bytes | Range |
|---|---|---|
| Boolean | Varies | True or False |
| Byte | 1 | 0 through 65535 (unsigned) |
| Char | 2 | 0 through 65535 (unsigned) (a single character) |
| Date | 8 | 0:00:00 midnight on Jan 1, 0001 to 11:59:59 Dec. 31, 9999 |
| Decimal | 16 | |
| Double | 8 | -1.79769313486231570E+308 through -4.94065645841246544E-324 for negative values 4.94065645841246544E-324 through 1.79769313486231570E+308 for positive values |
| Integer | 4 | -2,147,483,648 through 2,147,483,647 (signed) |
| Long | 8 | -9,223,372,036,854,775,808 through 9,223,372,036,854,775,807 |
| Object 32 bit | 4 | Any type can be stored in a variable of type Object |
| Object 64 bit | 8 | Any type can be stored in a variable of type Object |
| Sbyte | 1 | -128 through 127 (signed) |
| Short | 2 | -32,768 through 32,767 (signed) |
| Single | 4 | -3.4028235E+38 through -1.401298E-45 negative values 1.401298E-45 through 3.4028235E+38 positive values |
| String | Varies | 0 to approximately 2 billion Unicode values |

| Data Type | Bytes | Range |
|---|---|---|
| Uinteger | 4 | 0 through 4,294,967,295 (unsigned) |
| Ulong | 8 | 0 through 18,446,744,073,551,675 (unsigned) |
| User Defined (struct) | Varies | Type and independent of the ranges of the other members |
| Ushort | 2 | 0 though 65,535 (unsigned) |

It is important to understand the type of data being stored in a variable to insure the value being stored will never exceed the maximum or minimum stated values. This will cause an error and if the program does not check for storage errors, the program may terminate abnormally.

There are also composite data types like a structure or an array but these will be discussed as part of more advanced topics.

### 4.3   Declare Variables

Before you can use a variable it must be declared. This allows the compiler to set aside the proper amount of memory and attach the name you assigned to the variable to that storage location. The syntax for declaring a variable is:

**Dim** *variablename* **As** *DataType*

The statement starts with the keyword **Dim** (probably short for Dimension). Then the name of the variable, the name the programmer assigns to the storage area. Naming variables can be very important to easy to read and understand programs. We will discuss naming conventions in the next section. The name is followed by the keyword **As**. Then the DataType is assigned to the storage area.

To assign a variable to be used as a counter you could assign it as follows:

```
Dim intCounter As Integer
```

This assigns a storage area to hold an Integer value and it may be referred to as intCounter in the program code.

## 4.4 Variable Names

Giving your variables is an important part of programming and attention to the proper naming will help in coding and debugging your program. One of the great features of the Visual Basic IDE is something called "IntelleSense". This feature assists you in typing your code by suggesting values after typing the first two or three characters of a word. By assigning a prefix to your data name this can assist you in finding and properly spelling your variable as you type your code.

There are some rule for naming your variables that have been set by the compiler.

1. Variable names must begin with a letter.
2. Variable names may NOT contain a space.
3. After the first character the name may contain letters, numbers and the underscore (_) character.
4. Variable names may be up to 255 characters in length.
5. No reserved or keywords
6. Do not repeat variable names within the same level of scope.
7. Variable names are NOT case sensitive.

By using a pefix on the variable name, coding becomes easier. The prefix indicates the type of data stored in that variable. So when you look at a variable name it indicates the type of data stored. Also, when you type the prefix when coding, IntelleSense bring up a list of all the variables with that prefix. This helps with spelling and the typing of variable names.

Some of the prefixes you will be using in this course. Note there are other variables for which we have not noted prefixes and you may see other values for a prefix in other texts.

| Prefix | Data Type | Example |
|--------|-----------|---------|
| byt | Byte | bytCount |
| srt | Short | srtIndex |
| int | Integer | intHours |
| chr | Character | chrResponse |
| lng | Long | lngPopulation |
| sng | Single | sngPayRate |

| Prefix | Data Type | Example |
|--------|-----------|---------|
| dbl | Double | dblAnswer |
| dec | Decimal | decGrossPay |
| str | String | strMessage |
| dte | Date | dteStart |
| bln | Boolean | blnFinished |
| obj | Object | objBrush |

Use these prefixes and you will write better code and it will save you time in coding, debugging and maintenance.

Now examine some examples of valid and invalid variable names.

| VALID | INVALID |
|-------|---------|
| decPay_Rate | decPay Rate |
| intHours | int#Hours |
| blnComplete | 123Counter |
| strFullName | 7Eleven |
| dblFinish_Speed | dec Pay |
| srt123 | dbl%interest |

Before going any further, make sure you can identify why the invalid variable names are invalid.

## 4.5   TextBox Control

TextBox controls are used to accept data from the user.  TextBoxes are placed on the form and the user enters the requested data.  The program reads the data from the **text** property of the TextBox control.

42

## 4.5.1 Step-by-Step Exercise

Now it is time to practice using some of the controls we have learned in this and previous lessons.

Start a new project named "Calc"
Build a form that looks like the form in Figure 4.5.1.1

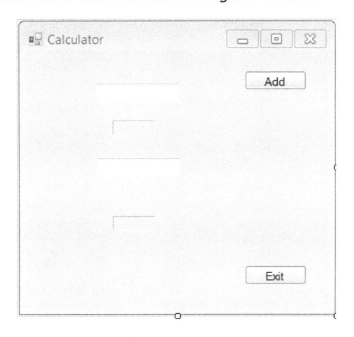

### *Figure 4.5.1.1*

Now we will assign proper values to the properties of the controls we have used. The next table shows the controls, the property and the value to be assigned to that property.

| Control | Property | Value |
| --- | --- | --- |
| Form1 | (Name) | frmCalc |
| Form1 | Text | Calculator |
| TextBox1 | (Name) | txtNum1 |
| TextBox2 | (Name) | txtNum2 |
| Label1 | (Name) | lblOper |
| Label1 | AutoSize | FALSE |

43

| Control | Property | Value |
| --- | --- | --- |
| Label1 | BorderStyle | Fixed3D |
| Label2 | (Name) | lblAns |
| Label2 | AutoSize | FALSE |
| Label2 | BorderStyle | Fixed3D |
| Button1 | (Name) | btnAdd |
| Button1 | Text | &Add |
| Button2 | (Name) | frmExit |
| Button2 | Text | E&xit |

Next, double-click on the button labeled "Calculate" to get to the code window event for btnCalc_Click event.

```
Public Class frmCalc

    Private Sub btnAdd_Click(ByVal sender As System.Object, ByVal e As System.EventArgs) Handles btnAdd.Click
        Dim intNum1 As Integer
        Dim intNum2 As Integer
        intNum1 = CInt(txtNum1.Text)
        intNum2 = CInt(txtNum2.Text)
        lblOper.Text = "+"
        lblAns.Text = intNum1 + intNum2
    End Sub

    Private Sub btnExit_Click(ByVal sender As System.Object, ByVal e As System.EventArgs) Handles btnExit.Click
        Me.Close()
    End Sub
End Class
```

**Figure 4.5.1.2**

Using the example in Figure 4.5.1.2, code the application. Again, make sure you avoid those blue and red squiggly lines by making sure you accurately name controls and write accurate code.

Compile and execute the program when you get a clean compile. Using some values for Num1 and Num2 make sure your calculator works.

The contents of the Text property of the TextBox may be cleared by using the Clear method:

```
txtHours.Clear()
```

This command clears the Text property of the control named txtHours.

## 4.6   Using Variables

Now that we have declared variables they can be used in code.  To be useful, a variable must have a value.  One way to load a value into a variable is to take the value from a textbox on the form.  In our example there is a textbox on the form named txtName.  We need to copy that value into a variable that can hold the data type of string.

```
Dim strName As String
strName = txtName.Text
```

This code declares a string variable and then copies the contents of the text property of the textbox named txtName into the string variable named strName.

Another way to get data into a variable is to load the variable with a literal.

```
Dim decRateOfPay As Decimal
decRateOfPay = 12.75
```

This command puts the value 12.75 into the variable named decRateOfPay.

The next code segment takes the contents of two variables and adds them together and stores the result in a third variable.

```
Dim intNumOne As Integer
Dim intNumTwo As Integer
Dim intAnswer As Integer

intNumOne = 15
intNumTwo = 30
intAnswer = intNumOne + intNumTwo
```

The three variables are declared and the first two are assigned values.  Then the final statement adds the contents of the variable intNumOne and the contents of the variable intNumTwo and stores the result in the variable intAnswer.  At the end of the operations the variable

45

intAnswer will contain the value 45 ( the sum of 15 + 30 ).

Variables may also be assigned values when they are declared.  The next code segment shows three variables being assigned and initialized to values.

```
Dim intNumOne As Integer = 21
Dim decPayRate As Decimal = 11.45
Dim strGreeting As String = "Hello, World!"
```

In taking values from the various controls on a form it is important to understand what properties in the form controls contain the data and how, in some cases, the data is to be converted to be stored in a variable in the code.

Two of the more common places to obtain numbers from the form are from textboxes and InputBoxes.  The textbox stores the value as a string in the text property of the control.  The InputBox returns a string when the user clicks on the OK button of the InputBox.

In both instances the data must be converted if it is to be used as a number in the code.  Visual Basic provides functions to do this conversion.  We will look at <u>two different</u> ways to accomplish the conversion.

### 4.7   Conversion of String Values to Numbers

There are several functions built in to the VB language to convert text data to other data types or convert other data types to string data. Data entered into text boxes is string data and if you need to do calculations on the entered data it must first be converted to the appropriate data type and stored in a variable of the same data type. Conversely, when a number is to be written by the program to a label or other form control, it also must be converted back to a string.

The following table shows some of the most often used conversion functions.

| Function | Description |
|----------|-------------|
| CDate(expr) | Converts a string to a valid date |
| CDbl(expr) | Converts an expression to a type Double |
| CDec(expr) | Converts an expression to a type Decimal |
| CInt(expr) | Converts an expression to a type Integer |

| Function | Description |
|----------|-------------|
| CStr(expr) | Converts an expression to a String |

To move the value in the Text property of a TextBox named txtGross, convert to a decimal value and store in a variable named decGrossPay, you would use the following command:

```
decGrossPay = CDbl(txtGross.Text)
```

Note that the CDbl Function is used with the argument as the text property of the textbox.

## 4.8  *Scope of Variables*

Scope of Variables refers to where a variable is created, and how long its contents are available to the program.  Every variable has scope, scope determines which part of a program in which a variable may be accessed.

Most of the variables we declare are "Local Variables".  This means that the variable exists with its contents until the code segments exit. The statement begins with the Dim statement within the event handler, module, function and sets aside the necessary memory to store a value of the designated type.  The value is retained in memory until the  event handler, module, or function exits.

If it is necessary to pass information in variables between event handlers, modules, and functions, a "Class Level Variable" is the answer.  A variable declared within a class but not inside a event handler is a class level variable.  All code segments within the Class have access to the variable and its contents.  The contents of the variable are not lost until the associated form is closed.

You declare a Class Level Variable as follows:

```
Public Class Form1
        Dim variablename AS dataType
Event Handlers
End Class
```

Since the variables are created when the form opens and they are cleared when the form closes, all event  handlers have access to these variables until the form closes.  Any event handler can read the variable or change the variable.

## 4.9 Constants

A constant is a category of variable that is given a value before the program is compiled, at code time, and the contents of that variable may not be changed except by recoding and recompiling.

Constants may be declared as Local Constants as well as Class Level Constants. These adhere to the same rules as Local variables and Class Level variables.

Constants are assigned values when they are declared. The syntax for declaring a constant is:

```
Const ConstantName As DataType = Value
```

Note that the syntax is the same as declaring a variable with the exception of replacing the keyword Dim with the keyword Const.

The next code segment shows three constants being declared.

```
ConstintNumOne As Integer = 21
Const decPayRate As Decimal = 11.45
Const strGreeting As String = "Hello, World!"
```

## 4.10 Summary

A variable is a storage place for information within the code. When the code needs to process data entered from a form, it is extracted from the form and stored in a designated storage place within the code area. Each data type reserves a certain amount of storage for each of these areas according to the type of data being stored.

There are rules for assigning user names to these storage areas and the programmer must follow these rules when assigning variable names. There is also the data type prefixes for variable names. While these are not rules they do provide assistance to the programmer when writing code.

The information provided from a TextBox or a InputBox() function is always text data. If it is a numeric value to be used in a calculation in the code, it must be converted to a different format. The lesson discussed two different ways to do this conversion.

The scope of variables determines how long the system will maintain the contents of a variable. A local variable is only availble for as long as the code segment in which it is defined, is active. Once the code segment closes, the contents are no longer available. Class Level variables are maintained as long as the form is open.

A specific type of variable called a constant is a little different.  A constant is a variable that is assigned a value at coding time and that value cannot be changed by the program.  It will still adhere to the rules of scope.  There may be local constants and Class Level constants.

# Lesson 5
# Calculations

## 5.1   Visual Basic Calculations

One of the more important tasks in many programming languages is the ability to calculate.  Visual Basic, like other programming languages, provide excellent arithmetic capabilities.   Addition, Subtraction, Multiplication, and Division are all available.   This lesson addresses using arithmetic in programs.

## 5.2  Arithmetic Operators

There are seven arithmetic operators.

| Operator | Used for |
|----------|----------|
| **+** | addition |
| **-** | subtraction |
| **\*** | multiplication |
| **/** | division |
| **\\** | integer division |
| **mod** | modulus (remainder) |
| **^** | exponentiation |

Addition, subtraction, multiplication, and division are used as in any arithmetic operation.  They will work for all numeric data.  Note there are other data types and it is important that you do not attempt these arithmetic operations on any other data type than numeric data types.

It is necessary to insure that when using data from the text property of a TextBox and the InputBox function, the entered data is to be converted to a numeric data type before any arithmetic operation is attempted.

## 5.3  Integer Division and Modulus

Visual Basic can process numeric data for division with and without decimals.  Normal division will account for all decimal positions with all data types that allow decimal positons.

Integers, by  definition, do not allow fractional data.  Integers are whole numbers only.  When integer division occurs, any fractional part (remainder) is lost.  The arithmetic operator for integer division is the backslash (\).  If the remainder is required, repeat the same division replacing the backslash (\) with the *mod* operator.

An example of where modulus may be used.  A warehouse has 137 units of a new product in their inventory.  They have instructed the warehouse to pack the units into cartons.  Each carton holds twelve units.  The program needs to calculate how many cartons  (137 \ 12) will be needed and how many units (137 mod 12) will be returned to inventory.

## 5.4  Label Controls

Label controls are used to place information on the form, both at design time and while the programming is running.  Good design principles dictate that any output from the program that is delivered to the form will be placed in a label control.

The label control displays the contents of the **text** property on the form.

Label controls should be named with the prefix lbl to indicate a label. If the label is being used for output it may have additional properties set.  The visible property may be set to FALSE to initially hide the control, and then made visible when a value is stored in the text property.  The AutoSize property set to FALSE and the BorderStyle property set to 3DFixed allow for a fixed size label where the space to show a label may be limited or a label may begin with and empty text property.

The code to place a the string "Hello, World!" in a label named lblGreet is:

```
lblGreet.Text = "Hello, World!"
```

To change the visible property to true:

```
lblGreet.Visible = True
```

AutoSize and BorderStyle properties should be set at design time.

## 5.5   Conversion and Input Validation

Often, just converting entered data is not sufficient for processing in a program.  It may be important to verify the data may be converted to the desired data type before conversion.  If the data does not convert properly, the program can send the user a message, allowing the user to correct the entry or end the program.  These functions convert the data exactly as the other built-in functions discussed in Section 4.6, but also allow the program to evaluate and send error messages when the data cannot be converted.

The following table shows some of the most often used conversion functions.

| Method | Description |
|---|---|
| Integer.TryParse | Accepts two arguments, the string to be converted and the integer variable. |
| Double.TryParse | Accepts two arguments, the string to be converted and the double variable. |
| Decimal.TryParse | Accepts two arguments, the string to be converted and the decimal variable. |
| Single.TryParse | Accepts two arguments, the string to be converted and the single variable. |
| Date.TryParse | Accepts two arguments, the string to be converted and the date variable. |

An example of using this type of validation.  The user enters data into a control named txtHours.  The program pulls the value from the text property and stores the value converted to a integer type value in a integer variable named intHours.  Since this does a comparison we must embed in an IF..THEN..ELSE statement.  If the value passes validation the TRUE expression will be executed.  If it fails validation the FALSE expression will be executed.

```
If Integer.TryParse(txtHours.Text, intHours) Then
    MessageBox.Show("Success!")
Else
    MessageBox.Show("Failure")
EndIf
```

If the user enters a valid Integer value the "Success!" message will be shown.  Anything that fails the integer test will generate the "Failure" message.

## 5.6  Assignment Operators

Assignment operators are a coding shortcut that may be used when a value is being added to another value where the variable receiving the calculated result is one of the operands.  EXAMPLE:  A variable named intCount needs to be incremented by 10.  The code would look like this:

```
intCount = intCount +1
```

Using assignment operators we could write this as:

```
intcount += 1
```

Both statements will give the same result.  Some of the assignment operators are in the table below.

| Operator | Description | Example |
|---|---|---|
| ( = ) | Simple Assignment Operator | x = 5 + 9 |
| ( += ) | ADD And Assignment Operator.  Adds the right operand to the left operand and stores the result in the left operand. | intCount += 1<br><br>increases intCount by 1 |
| ( -= ) | SUBTRACT And Assignment Operator. Subtracts the right operand from the left operand and stores the result in the left operand. | intCount -= 1<br><br>decrements intCount by 1 |
| ( *= ) | MULTIPLY And Assignment Operator. Multiplies the right operand by the left operand and stores the result in the left operand. | decNum1 *= decNum2<br><br>Multiplies the value in decNum1 by the value in decNum2 |
| ( /= ) | DIVISION And Assignment Operator. Divides the right operand into the left operand and stores the result in the left operand. | decNum1 /= decNum2<br><br>Divides the value in decNum1 by the value in decNum2 |
| ( \= ) | INTEGER DIVISION And Assignment Operator.  Divides the right operand into the left operand and stores the result in the left operand. | intNum1 \= intNum2<br><br>Integer divides the value in decNum1 by the value in decNum2 |

| Operator | Description | Example |
|---|---|---|
| ( ^= ) | EXPONENTIATION And Assignment Operator. Raises the left operand to the power of the right operand and stores the result in the left operand. | IntNum1 ^= intNum2<br><br>Raises the value in decNum1 to the power indicated in decNum2 |
| ( .= ) | CONCATENATES a String Expression to a String variable and assigns the result to the variable | str1 .= strName |

## 5.7   Create a Calculator

Using the project "Calc" created in Step by Step 5.5.1.

Add the following functions and program them using what you have learned to this point in the course.

    Subtract
    Multiply
    Divide
    Integer Divide
    Modulus

I recommend that you add these operations one at a time, get one working and then move on to the next.

Test all of your operations with several different values and make sure the calculated values are correct.

## 5.8   Summary

The computer is the ultimate calculator. It handles numbers very efficiently. This lesson showed how to use this power in an application program. There are seven arithmetic operators.

The controls on the form addressed in this lesson were the TextBox and the Label. The TextBox control is where the user of the form can enter data. The data is stored in the Text Property of the control as a string value. If it is a number that will be used in a calculation, it must be converted to a numeric value of the correct data type.

Labels are used to display program calculations, messages, to describe a text box or give instructions.

# Lesson 6
## Strings, Formatting Numbers and the MessageBox.

### 6.1 Strings and String Variables

A string is a group of zero or more characters. A string with zero characters is known as a NULL string. We generally think of a string as a sentence, a name, a combination of letters, numbers and special characters or a group of characters that includes spaces.
All data entered into a TextBox or InputBox is stored as a string.

As we learned in Lesson 4 a string variable is declared as follows

```
Dim stringname As String
```

To declare a string that would hold the name of an employee the statement may look something like this:

```
Dim strEmployeeName As String
```

Additionally we could initialize the string variable to a value like this:

```
Dim strEmployeeName As String = "Jon Dough"
```

To code a statement that will assign a value to a string variable the code would be:

```
strEmployeeName = "Mary Smith"
```

This code would result in the string literal "Mary Smith" replacing the previous contents of the string variable named strEmployeeName.

To move the contents of the string variable strEmployeeName to a label on the form named lblName the following code is required:

```
lblName.Text = strEmployeeName
```

Note that no data conversion is required to write a string into a Property of a control.

### 6.1.1 Step-by-Step Exercise

This exercise will produce a form that will accept a name entered into a TextBox and then copy the name to a label.

Create a new project named StringCopy.

Create a form that looks like Figure 6.1.1.1
Name the form frmName – Text property should be COPY NAME
Name the text box txtName

Name the label lblName  Text property blank
AutoSize property should be False
BorderStyle should be Fixed3D
Name the first button btnReset – Text property should be RESET
Name the second button btnCopy – Text property should be COPY

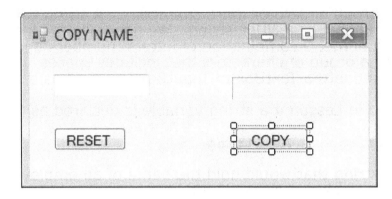

*Figure 6.6.1.1*

Double click on the RESET button and enter the two lines of code shown for the btnReset_Click event in Figure 6.6.1.2.

Double-click on the COPY button and enter the single line of code shown for the btnCopy_Click event in Figure 6.6.1.2.

```
Public Class frmName

    Private Sub btnReset_Click(ByVal sender As System.Object, ByVal e As System.EventArgs) Handles btnRese
        lblName.Text = " "
        txtName.Text = " "
    End Sub

    Private Sub btnCopy_Click(ByVal sender As System.Object, ByVal e As System.EventArgs) Handles btnCopy.
        lblName.Text = txtName.Text
    End Sub
End Class
```

*Figure 6.6.1.2*

Now compile the application and when there is a clean compile test the program.

Enter your name in the text box.
Click on the COPY button
Your name should now be in the label named lblName
Click on the RESET button
Both the textbox and the label should be blank.
Enter your best friends name in the text box
Click on the COPY button
Click on the RESET button

56

## *6.2 Concatenation*

Often there may be more than one string that needs to be put together to form a complete string. We will make some modifications to our program to allow a first name and a last name to be entered. The output will be built by creating a string composed of the first name, a space, and the last name.

The concatenation character is the & (ampersand). Older versions of Basic used the + sign but that symbol is no longer valid for concatenating strings.

## 6.6.2 Step-by-Step Exercise

Open the StringCopy project if it is not already open.

Make the changes shown in the form that are shown in Figure 6.6.2.1

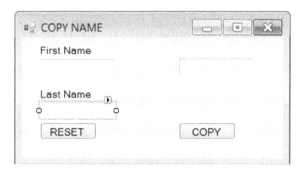

## *Figure 6.6.2.1*

Make the changes to the code as indicated below. Note the code for the event btnCopy_Click has been completely changed.

> A variable named strFullName is declared.
> The variable is assigned two strings and a string literal
> > string 1 is from txtName.Text
> > > string literal " " to put a space between the two strings.
> > > String 2 is from txtLName.Text

57

```
Public Class frmName

    Private Sub btnReset_Click(ByVal sender As System.Object, ByVal e As System.EventArgs) Handles btnRese
        lblName.Text = " "
        txtName.Text = " "
        txtLName.Text = " "
    End Sub

    Private Sub btnCopy_Click(ByVal sender As System.Object, ByVal e As System.EventArgs) Handles btnCopy.
        Dim strFullName As String
        strFullName = txtName.Text & " " & txtLName.Text
        lblName.Text = strFullName
    End Sub
End Class
```

**Figure 6.6.2.2**

Strings cannot be used in a calculation until they have been converted into a numeric data type recognized by Visual Basic (See Lesson 4.6 Conversion of String Values to Numbers). Strings are usually stored in either ASCII or UniCode formats.

Once the information has been entered it can be converted into the appropriate data type and stored in the program for future operations. Once the operations have been completed, it is usually necessary to display the results of the calculations either on the screen, in print or saved to a file. When the output is visible, it is important to format the output in a format that assists the viewer in understanding the value represented.

### 6.3   The Decimal Data Type

When dealing with fractional parts of numbers, the type Double comes to mind. Type Double efficiently handles numbers with fractional parts, handling them as whole number plus a decimal part that represents the fractional part.

There is also a data type called Decimal. The Decimal data type is designed for storing Currency. The difference between Decimal and Double is that Decimal is more accurate when dealing with dollars and cents. The recommendation is that when dealing with Currency amounts, use the Decimal data type.

## 6.4 Formatting a number

Formatting numbers is accomplished using the ToString() function. The ToString() function requires a numeric format string as a parameter. The numeric format strings are as follows:

| Format String | Description |
|---|---|
| N or n | Number Format |
| F or f | Fixed-Point Scientific Format |
| E or e | Exponential Scientific format |
| C or c | Currency Format |
| P or p | Percent Format |

The syntax for using the ToString method is as follows:

decPayRate.ToString("c")

Each numeric string may be followed by an optional integer to indicate the number of places after the decimal point (precision). For Example if the number 123.356 is stored in a variable dblAverage.

dblNewAvg = dblAverage.ToString("n2")

The result will be the value 123.36 stored in dblNewAvg. Note that the number was rounded up since the last digit 6 was equal to or greater than 5.

An integer may be displayed with the D or d Format String. This will allow integers to be displayed with leading zeros.

| Integer | Format String | Formatted As |
|---|---|---|
| 12 | D | 12 |
| 12 | D4 | 0012 |
| 1 | D2 | 01 |

Dates and Times may also be formatted. The Date data type holds a numeric date and time but that date and/or time may then be formatted into a number of different formats.

| Format String | Description |
| --- | --- |
| d | Short Date Format "8/3/2014" |
| D | Long Date Format "Sunday, August 3, 2014" |
| t | Short Time Format "4:10 PM" |
| T | Long Time Format "4:10:45 PM" |
| F | Full Date and Time<br><br>"Sunday, August 3, 2014 4:10:45 PM" |

To create a string containing "8/3/2014":

```
Dim dteToday As Date "#8/3/2014#"
Dim strResult As String
strResult = dteToday.ToString("d")
```

Note the date string literal encloses the date in a pair of pound signs (#). This is required to indicate that the string is to be interpreted as a date or date time value.

## 6.6   MessageBox.Show Method

The MessageBox.Show method is a way for the program to communicate a message to the user. It will show a dialog box containing a message to the user. The user answers the message by clicking on the OK button.

***Figure 6.6.1***

The messagebox shown in Figure 6.6.1 was displayed by code using the statement:

```
MessageBox.Show("Microsoft Visual Basic")
```

The MessageBox.Show method contains a string literal in the set of parenthesis. This is the string that is displayed in the messagebox in Figure 6.6.1. The messagebox is closed by clicking on the OK button.

## 6.6.1 Step-by-Step Exercise

Create a form that looks like the form in Figure 6.6.1.1 below.

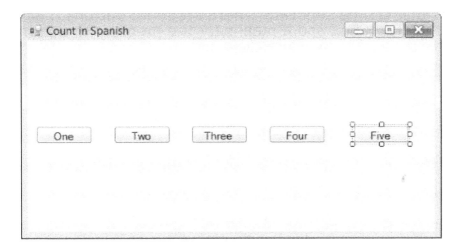

*Figure 6.6.1.1*

Now code each button as shown in Figure 6.6.1.2

```
Public Class frmCount

    Private Sub btnOne_Click(ByVal sender As System.Object, ByVal e As System.EventArgs) Handles btnOne.Click
        MessageBox.Show("UNO")
    End Sub

    Private Sub btnTwo_Click(ByVal sender As System.Object, ByVal e As System.EventArgs) Handles btnTwo.Click
        MessageBox.Show("DOS")
    End Sub

    Private Sub btnThree_Click(ByVal sender As System.Object, ByVal e As System.EventArgs) Handles btnThree.Click
        MessageBox.Show("TRES")
    End Sub

    Private Sub btnFour_Click(ByVal sender As System.Object, ByVal e As System.EventArgs) Handles btnFour.Click
        MessageBox.Show("CUATRO")
    End Sub

    Private Sub btnFive_Click(ByVal sender As System.Object, ByVal e As System.EventArgs) Handles btnFive.Click
        MessageBox.Show("CINCO")
    End Sub
End Class
```

*Figure 6.6.1.2*

Now make sure you do not have any obvious errors and compile the application.

When the application complies clean and runs, test each of the buttons to make sure you get the correct results.

## 6.7 More About MessageBox.Show Method

The MessageBox.Show method is actually a little more programmable than we discovered in the last section. There are number of other parameters that can be supplied. There are more buttons that can be placed on the dialog box and a means for the program to determine which one of those buttons were clicked.

The full syntax for the MessageBox.Show Method are as follows:

```
MessageBox.Show(Message)
MessageBox.Show(Message, Caption)
MessageBox.Show(Message, Caption, Buttons)
MessageBox.Show(Message, Caption, Buttons, Icon)
MessageBox.Show(Message, Caption, Buttons, Icon,
DefaultBtn)
```

**Message** – The message to be displayed in the message area of the dialog box. If you wish to display multiple lines of information in a MesageBox, use the constant ControlChars.CrLf  (CrLf stands for Carriage Return Line Feed)

```
MessageBox.Show("This is Line 1" & ControlChars.CrLf &
            "This is Line 2")
```

**Caption** – This string will be displayed in the top left corner of the dialog box.

**Buttons** – Tells what combination of buttons are to be displayed.

```
MessageBoxButtons.AbortRetryIgnore
    Displays:  Abort Retry Ignore Buttons
MessageBoxButtons.OK
    Displays:  OK Button
MessageBoxButtons.OKCancel
    Displays:  OK Cancel Buttons
MessageBoxButtons.RetryCancel
    Displays:  Retry Cancel Buttons
MessageBoxButtons.YesNo
    Displays:  Yes No Buttons
MessageBoxButtons.YesNoCancel
    Displays:  Yes No Cancel Buttons
```

**Icon** – An Icon that is in front of the message that gives a visual cue on the nature of the message.

       MessageBoxIcon.Asterisk
       MessageBoxIcon.Information
       MessageBoxIcon.Error
       MessageBoxIcon.Hand
       MessageBoxIcon.Stop
       MessageBoxIcon.Exclamation
       MessageBoxIcon.Warning
       MessageBoxIcon.Question

**DefaultBtn** – Indicates the button position that will  be the default button.  The default button is clicked when the user presses the Enter Key.

       MessageBoxDefaultButton.Button1
       MessageBoxDefaultButton.Button2
       MessageBoxDefaultButton.Button3

The program can also determine which of the buttons were clicked. The code required to capture this information is:
       Windows.Forms.DialogResult.Abort
       Windows.Forms.DialogResult.Cancel
       Windows.Forms.DialogResult.Ignore
       Windows.Forms.DialogResult.No
       Windows.Forms.DialogResult.OK
       Windows.Forms.DialogResult.Retry
       Windows.Forms.DialogResult.Yes

Determining which button the user has clicked is part of our lesson on making decisions (Lesson 7).

### 6.8   Formatting numbers program.

Create a new project named FormatNumbers and build the form as shown in Figure 6.8.1.

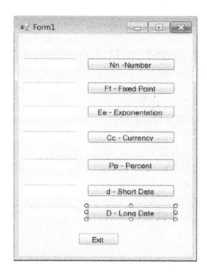

**Figure 6.8.1**

Change the control properties as shown in the following table:

| Control | Property |
|---|---|
| TextBox1 | (Name) = txtNum |
| Button1 | (Name) = btnNum |
|  | Text = Nn - Number |
| TextBox2 | (Name) = txtFixed |
| Button2 | (Name) = btnFixed |
|  | Text = Ff - Fixed-Point |
| TextBox3 | (Name) = txtExponent |
| Button3 | (Name) = btnExponent |
|  | Text = Ee - Exponentation |
| TextBox4 | (Name) = txtCurrency |
| Button4 | (Name) = btnCurrency |

| Control | Property |
|---|---|
| | Text = Cc - Currency |
| TextBox5 | (Name) = txtPercent |
| Button5 | (Name) = btnPercent |
| | Text = Pp – Percent |
| TextBox6 | (Name) = txtSDate |
| Button6 | (Name) = btnSDate |
| | Text = d - Short Date |
| TextBox7 | (Name) = txtLDate |
| Button7 | (Name) = btnLDate |
| | Text = D – Long Date |

Once the form is complete enter the code shown in Figure 6.8.2

```
    Private Sub btnNum_Click(ByVal sender As System.Object, ByVal
e As System.EventArgs) Handles btnNum.Click
        Dim intNum As Integer

        intNum = CInt(txtNum.Text)

        MessageBox.Show(intNum.ToString("N"))

    End Sub



    Private Sub btnFixed_Click(ByVal sender As System.Object, ByVal e As
System.EventArgs) Handles btnFixed.Click

        Dim dblNum As Double

        dblNum = CDbl(txtFixed.Text)

        MessageBox.Show(dblNum.ToString("F"))

    End Sub
```

```vb
    Private Sub btnExponent_Click(ByVal sender As System.Object, ByVal e As
System.EventArgs) Handles btnExponent.Click

        Dim dblNum As Double

        dblNum = CDbl(txtExponent.Text)

        MessageBox.Show(dblNum.ToString("E"))

    End Sub


    Private Sub btnCurrency_Click(ByVal sender As System.Object, ByVal e As
System.EventArgs) Handles btnCurrency.Click

        Dim decNum As Decimal

        decNum = CDec(txtCurrency.Text)

        MessageBox.Show(decNum.ToString("C"))

    End Sub


    Private Sub btnPercent_Click(ByVal sender As System.Object, ByVal e As
System.EventArgs) Handles btnPercent.Click

        Dim dblNum As Double

        dblNum = CDbl(txtPercent.Text)

        MessageBox.Show(dblNum.ToString("P"))

    End Sub


    Private Sub btnSDate_Click(ByVal sender As System.Object, ByVal e As
System.EventArgs) Handles btnSDate.Click

        Dim dteNum As Date

        dteNum = CDate(txtSDate.Text)

        MessageBox.Show(dteNum.ToString("d"))

    End Sub


    Private Sub btnLDate_Click(ByVal sender As System.Object, ByVal e As
System.EventArgs) Handles btnLDate.Click

        Dim dteNum As Date

        dteNum = CDate(txtLDate.Text)
```

```
MessageBox.Show(dteNum.ToString("D"))

End Sub
```

### Figure 6.8.2

When the code is complete, run the program using the following values to test each condition in the program. Note, there are two test runs for the program. Your program should match the results. Examine the code to insure you understand why that code produced the results.

| Button | Test#1 | Result#1 | Test#2 | Result#2 |
|---|---|---|---|---|
| Nn - Number | 12345.22 | | 12345.82 | |
| Ff – Fixed | 12345.22 | | 12345.82 | |
| Ee - Exponentation | 1234.567 | | 12.34567 | |
| Cc – Currency | 12.45 | | 33 | |
| Pp - Percent | 0.12 | | 0.875 | |
| d – Short Date | 08/04/14 | | August 5, 2014 | |
| D – Long Date | 08/04/14 | | August 5, 2014 | |

## 6.9   Summary

Strings are groups of characters (ASCII or UNICODE) that represent numbers, letters, special characters that can be displayed to the computer screen or printed output. Visual Basic supports a string data type for variables, that may hold 0 to approximately 2 billion Unicode Characters.

Strings cannot be used in a calculation until they have been converted into a numeric data type recognized by Visual Basic. Data input into TextBoxes is stored in the Text property as a String or also called text data.

Text or String data must be converted into numbers before any calculations can take place. When the calculations are complete the numbers must be converted back into text / string data before being sent to the text property of a label or used in a message displayed by the MessageBox.Show method.

Numbers displayed properly are displayed according to the type of number displayed. A currency value should be displayed with a preceding $ (dollar sign). A percent value follwed by a % (percent sign). Numbers in the thousands should have a properly placed comma and decimal portions should be rounded properly.

The MessageBox.Show method is a way to communicate to the user. It builds a dialog box and displays a message to the user. For the simple MessageBox there is a message and a OK button. The OK button is used to close the MessageBox.

The MessageBox can be expanded and show in addition to the message, a dialog box caption, an icon to identify the type of message, and a range of buttons that can be tested by the program to determine which choice the user selected. This will be discussed in the next lesson.

## Unit Three – Decisions and Repetition

Lesson 7 – Decisions

Lesson 8 – Repetition (Looping)

Lesson 9 - Arrays

# Lesson 7
# Decisions

## 7.1   Decisions

An important part of Visual Basic is the ability to evaluate the data and make decisions on how data will be processed.  If an evaluation of data results in a true decision, one set of code will be processed.  If the evaluation is false, a second set of code will be processed.  The expressions evaluated are know as Boolean Expressions.  A boolean expression can evaluate to only true or false.  An example is 5 > 1 (read 5 is greater than 1).  The answer can only be true or false.  Five is either greater than one or it is not greater (implies less than or equal to as false conditions).

## 7.2   Conditional Operators

There are six (6) conditional operators.  These allow for comparison of two operands.  An operand is a literal, variable or arithmetic expresson.  The following table (Table 7.2.1) shows the six conditional operators:

| Condition | Operator | Example |
|-----------|----------|---------|
| Equal | ( = ) | 5 = 5 |
| Not equal | ( <> ) | 3 != 5 |
| Greater than | ( > ) | 5 > 3 |
| Less than | ( < ) | 3 < 5 |
| Greater than or equal to | ( >= ) | 5 >= 4 |
| Less than or equal to | (<= ) | 3 <= 3 |

### Table 7.2.1

Note the conditions "Greater than or equal to", Less than or equal to", and "Not equal" all have two symbols.  Note the order of those symbols as they must always appear in the order shown in the table.

70

Each of the examples in Table 7.2.1, show a boolean expression that evaluates to true.

The next table (Table 7.2.2) shows examples of boolean expressions that evaluate to false.

| Condition | Operator | Example |
|---|---|---|
| Equal | ( = ) | 5 = 6 |
| Not equal | ( <> ) | 3 != 3 |
| Greater than | ( > ) | 5 > 8 |
| Less than | ( < ) | 8 < 5 |
| Greater than or equal to | ( >= ) | 5 >= 7 |
| Less than or equal to | (<= ) | 7 <= 3 |

*Table 7.2.2*

The examples in Table 7.2.2 show boolean expressions using literals as operands.  It is more common that the operands are variables or a combination of variables and literals.  Other examples of conditional expressions may be:

Variables used in Table 7.2.3 and their values:

intHours = 33                    chrResponse = 'Y'
intMaxHours = 40                 strGreet = "HI"
decPayRate = 12.70
decMaxPayRate = 27.45
decMinPayRate = 7.45

71

| Example | Evaluates to |
|---------|--------------|
| intHours < intMaxHours | True |
| decPayRate >= decMaxPayRate | False |
| decMinPayRate <= 6.50 | False |
| chrResponse = 'Y' | True |
| strGreet = "Hello" | False |

*Table 7.2.3*

The program uses these boolean expressions in decision statements to determine the code path the program should take.  Next, we take a look at these statements.

## 7.3   The If...Then Statement

The If...Then statement is a single sided IF statement.  The boolean expression is evaluated and if it evaluates to true the code within the if ...then statement are executed and when the condition evaluates to false, the structure is exited and continues with the statement after the EndIf statement.  The code within the if statement is only executed when the boolean expression tests true.

SYNTAX:

```
If [boolean expression] Then
     [statements to be executed only if the  boolean
          expression tests TRUE]
EndIf
```

If the boolean expression tests false the instruction that follows the EndIf instruction is executed.

### 7.3.1 Step-by-Step Exercise

Create a new project named "Password"

Create a form as shown in Figure 7.3.1.1

*Figure 7.3.1.1*

Next change the Properties as follows:

| Control | Property | Value |
|---------|----------|-------|
| Form1 | (Name) | frmPassword |
|  | Text | Password Check |
| Label1 | Text | Enter Your Password |
| TextBox1 | (Name) | txtPassword |
| Button1 | (Name) | btnPassword |
|  | Text | &Submit |

Once the properties have been changed, it is time to write the program.  Insert the code shown in Figure 7.3.1.2 in the proper place in your code area.

73

```
Public Class frmPassword

    Private Sub btnSubmit_Click(ByVal sender As System.Object, ByVal e As System.EventArgs) Handles btnSubmit.Click
        Dim strPass As String
        strPass = txtPassword.Text
        If strPass = "QWERTY12" Then
            MessageBox.Show("Password is Correct")
        End If
        MessageBox.Show("Program will Terminate")
    End Sub
End Class
```

### Figure 7.3.1.2

Now, if there are no errors test your program. Enter "ABC123" to test the boolean test FALSE outcome.

Enter "QWERTY12" to test the boolean test TRUE outcome.

## 7.4    The If...Then...Else Statement

The If...Then...Else statement tests a boolean expression and if it tests true it does one set of code, if the expression tests false the statements after the Else statement is executed.

SYNTAX:

```
If [boolean expression] Then
     [statements to be executed only if the  boolean
          expression tests TRUE]
Else
     [statements to be executed only if the boolean
          expression test FALSE]
EndIf
```

If the boolean expression tests True, the statements before the Else keyword are executed. When they have completed the next instruction executed is the instruction after the EndIf statement.

If the boolean expression tests False, the statements after the Else keyword are executed. When completed, the instruction after the EndIf statement is the next statement executed.

### 7.4.1.1 Step-by-Step Exercise

Create an new project named "Vote"

Place controls on a form so that it looks like the form shown in Figure 7.4.1.1. Then make sure you change all of the properties for the controls as they are listed below.

74

| Control | Property | Value |
| --- | --- | --- |
| Form1 | (Name) | frmVote |
|  | Text | Voter Registration |
| Label1 | Text | Enter Your Age: |
| TextBox1 | (Name) | txtAge |
| Button1 | (Name) | BtnCheck |
|  | Text | Check |
| Label2 | (Name) | lblReply |
|  | Visible | FALSE |

*Figure 7.4.1.1*

Once all properties have been changed go to the code window and enter the code as shown below in Figure 7.4.1.2.

```
Public Class frmVote

    Private Sub btnCheck_Click(ByVal sender As System.Object, ByVal e As System.EventArgs) Handles btnCheck.Click
        Dim intAge As Integer
        intAge = CInt(txtAge.Text)
        If intAge >= 18 Then
            lblReply.Text = "You May Vote!"
        Else
            lblReply.Text = "You Are Too Young To Vote!"
        End If
        lblReply.Visible = True
    End Sub
End Class
```

**Figure 7.4.1.2**

Make sure all code is entered correctly and compile the application.

Now you are ready to test.  Test your application three times using the following values:

Test #1 use the age 18 – Result: You May Vote!

Test #2 use the age 21 -  Result: You May Vote!

Test #3 use the age 16 – Result: You Are Too Young To Vote!

Did you receive the expected results?

## 7.5   Checkboxes

Checkboxes are used on forms to allow the user to select one or more items.  The user can select as many or as few as necessary.  The check mark in the box indicates that the IsChecked property is set to TRUE, conversely if not checked the IsChecked property  is set to FALSE.   The program can examine the IsChecked property to determine if the item has been selected.

### 7.5.1 Step-by-Step Exercise

Create a New project and name the project OperSys

Put the controls on the form so that it looks line the Form in Figure 7.5.1.1.

Change the properties for the controls as indicated below.

*Figure 7.5.1.1*

Name the Control properties as follows:

| Control | Property | Value |
| --- | --- | --- |
| Form1 | (Name) | FrmCheck |
|  | Text | Checkbox Demo |
| Checkbox1 | (Name) | ChkWin8 |
|  | Text | Windows 8 |
| Checkbox2 | (Name) | ChkWin7 |
|  | Text | Windows 7 |
| Checkbox3 | (Name) | ChkMAC |
|  | Text | MAC |
| Checkbox4 | (Name) | ChkLinux |
|  | Text | Linux |

| Control | Property | Value |
| --- | --- | --- |
| Checkbox5 | (Name) | ChkChrome |
|  | Text | Chrome |
| Label1 | Text | Select Operating System(s) for Information |
| Label 2 | (Name) | lblMessage |
|  | Visible | FALSE |

After all control properties have been changed go to the code window and program the click event for the GO button as shown in Figure 7.5.1.2.

```
Public Class frmCheck

    Private Sub btnGO_Click(ByVal sender As System.Object, ByVal e As System.EventArgs) Handles btnGO.Click
        Dim strMessage As String
        If chkWin8.Checked Then
            strMessage = "Windows 8"
        End If
        If chkWin7.Checked Then
            strMessage &= " Windows 7"
        End If
        strMessage &= ControlChars.CrLf
        If chkMAC.Checked Then
            strMessage &= "MAC OS/X"
        End If
        If chkLinux.Checked Then
            strMessage &= "Linux"
        End If
        If chkChrome.Checked Then
            strMessage &= "Chrome"
        End If
        lblMessage.Text = strMessage
        lblMessage.Visible = True
    End Sub
End Class
```

**Figure 7.5.1.2**

Now test your programs by testing several combinations of checkboxes.

## 7.6 Nested If statements

If statements can be placed within other If statements to test multiple conditions or make decisions based on several evaluations.

A simple example would be a program that evaluates a voter's eligibility to vote in an election. By rule the voter must be 18 year of age and registered to vote before they are allowed to vote. The If statement might look something like this:

```
If intAge => 18 Then
        If chkRegistered = 'Y' Then
                MessageBox.Show("You May Vote")
        Else
                MessageBox.Show("You need to register to vote")
    Else
            MessageBox.Show("You are too young to vote")
    EndIf
```

Nested if may exist on the true side, false side or both sides if necessary. Caution, nesting too many times may result in a hard to debug and maintain program.

### 7.6.1 Step-by-Step Exercise

Using the Step-by-Step created in Lesson 7.4, modify the form shown in Figure 7.4.1.1 to include a checkbox named chkRegistered. The box should be labeled "Check if Registered".

Then in the code as shown in Figure 7.4.1.2 change the IF statement to the following:

```
If intAge => 18 Then
        If chkRegistered = 'Y' Then
            MessageBox.Show("You May Vote")
        Else
            MessageBox.Show("You need to register to
vote")
    Else
        MessageBox.Show("You are too young to vote")
    EndIf
```

Test your new code to insure all of the conditions are handled properly.

## 7.7  *Logical Operators*

Logical operators can be used to combine several boolean expressions into a single expression.  The three most common logical operators are: Not, And, Or.  The following table describes how they are used.

| Operator | Description |
|---|---|
| Not | Reverses the outcome |
| And | All expressions or values connected by the AND operator must be TRUE for the result to be TRUE, any combination of TRUE and FALSE result in FALSE. |
| Or | Only one of the expressions or values connected by the OR operator must be TRUE for the result to be TRUE. |

Boolean Truth Tables for AND / OR

| AND | | | OR | |
|---|---|---|---|---|
| TEST | RESULT | | TEST | RESULT |
| T & T | T | | T & T | T |
| T & F | F | | T & F | T |
| F & T | F | | F & T | T |
| F & F | F | | F & F | F |

EXAMPLE

```
if (intX > 0) AND (intX < 10) Then
    MsgBox("Number Entered is within range")
EndIf
```

The AND operator only returns TRUE if BOTH operands are True. The OR operator only returns FALSE if both operands test False.

### 7.7.1 Step-by-Step Exercise

Then in the code changed in Step-by-Step 7.6.1. change the IF statement to the following:

```
If intAge => 18 And chkRegistered = 'Y' Then
        MessageBox.Show("You May Vote")
Else
    MessageBox.Show("You May NOT Vote")
EndIf
```

If the age is equal to or greater than 18 and the voter is registered, the message "You May Vote" will be displayed. If either of those tests return a condition of False, the message "You May NOT Vote" is returned.

## 7.8   Radio Buttons

Radio Buttons are similar to CheckBoxes. The main differences is that Radio Buttons only allow one choice. So if you place your Radio Buttons directly on a form, you can only select one radio button on the entire form. If it is necessary to use Radio Buttons for more than one selection, you must put the Radio Buttons in a GroupBox control. It is advisable to group Radio Buttons into GroupBox controls regardless of how you intend to use Radio Buttons.

A GroupBox control is a container for other controls. The controls inside a GroupBox are treated as one unit. Controls contained within the GroupBox are part of the control and move with the control and can be deleted by deleting the GroupBox.

The two most important properties of the GroupBox are the (Name) property and the Text property. The (Name) property designates a name that is associated with the control and is important when coding solutions. The Text property is displayed in the top left corner of the top border of the group box and can be used to label the group box to clarify the purpose of the contents of the GroupBox.

When Radio Buttons are used on a form, the following steps should be followed to create the GroupBox and the Radio Buttons to be contained in the GroupBox.

1. Create a GroupBox control on the form to hold the Radio Buttons.
2. Name the GroupBox appropriately in the (Name) property.
3. Put an appropriate label in the Text Property of the GroupBox.

4. Create Radio Buttons within the GroupBox.
5. Name the Radio Buttons appropriately and insert labels in the text property of each button.

When naming the GroupBox use the grp prefix and name the Radio Buttons using the rad prefix. (Note: you may also use the opt prefix for Radio Buttons).

## 7.8.1 Step-by-Step Exercise

Program Showing **Currency Exchange Rates**

Create a new project named Conversion

Build the form with controls as shown in Figure 7.8.1.1

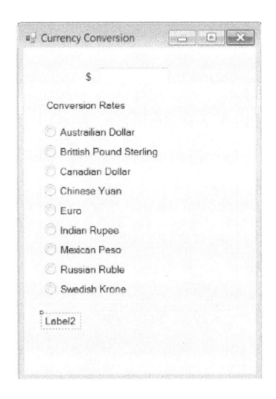

*Figure 7.8.1.1*

The text box (Name) property should be txtDollar and the label (Name) property should be lblCalc.

Names and text properties for the radio buttons are listed in the table below.  The group box containing the radio buttons has a text property of "Conversion Rates".

The partial code is contained in Figure 7.8.1.2.  You complete the code for the remaining radio buttons.

| Currency | Rate | Name Property |
|---|---|---|
| Australian Dollar | 1.07 | radAus |
| British Pound Sterling | .58 | radPound |
| Canadian Dollar | 1.08 | radCdn |
| Chinese Yuan | 6.20 | radYuan |
| Euro | .74 | radEuro |
| Indian Rupee | 60.07 | radRupee |
| Mexican Peso | 12.95 | radPeso |
| Russian Ruble | 34.40 | radRuble |
| Swedish Krone | 6.84 | radKrone |

```
Public Class Form1
    Dim strMessage As String
    Dim decDollar As Decimal


    Private Sub radAus_CheckedChanged(ByVal sender As System.Object, ByVal e As System.EventArgs) Handles radAus.CheckedChanged
        decDollar = CDec(txtDollar.Text) * 1.07
        strMessage = "Australian Dollar: " & decDollar.ToString("C")
        lblConv.Text = strMessage
    End Sub

    Private Sub radPound_CheckedChanged(ByVal sender As System.Object, ByVal e As System.EventArgs) Handles radPound.CheckedChanged
        decDollar = CDec(txtDollar.Text) * 0.58
        strMessage = "British Pound Sterling: " & decDollar.ToString("C")
        lblConv.Text = strMessage
    End Sub

    Private Sub radCdn_CheckedChanged(ByVal sender As System.Object, ByVal e As System.EventArgs) Handles radCdn.CheckedChanged
        decDollar = CDec(txtDollar.Text) * 1.08
        strMessage = "Canadian Dollar: " & decDollar.ToString("C")
        lblConv.Text = strMessage
    End Sub

    Private Sub radYuan_CheckedChanged(ByVal sender As System.Object, ByVal e As System.EventArgs) Handles radYuan.CheckedChanged
        decDollar = CDec(txtDollar.Text) * 6.2
        strMessage = "Chinese Yuan: " & decDollar.ToString("C")
        lblConv.Text = strMessage
    End Sub
End Class
```

**Figure 7.8.1.2**

Once the code is complete and error free, test the various options. I suggest entering One Dollar (1) as the dolllar amount and then test each button noting the display to insure the correct statement is output.

Coding Radio Buttons forces the programmer to concentrate on true event driven programming. When a radio button is clicked, this is an event. Something should happen when the button is clicked. VB handles placing the dot in the selected button and, if necessary, changing another control in the GroupBox. The programmer needs to create code for the Radio Button's CheckChanged Event.

## 7.9    Using Select Case Statement

If...Then statements handle one-way decisions. If...Then...Else statements handle two-way decisions. Then Nesting If statements allow the programmer to make decisions that branch in more than two paths. Perhaps an easier solution to the nesting for multiple paths is the Select Case statement.

The Select Case statement allows the programmer to specify a variable and then test for multiple values of the variable. If a variable has 9 possible values, a select case statement is an easier and more readable way to test this range of values.

84

```
Select Case intAge
    Case 0 To 2
        lblMsg.Text = "Infant"
    Case 3 To 5
        lblMsg.Text = "Toddler"
    Case 6 To 12
        lblMsg.Text = "Child"
    Case 13 to 19
        lblMsg.Text = "Teen"
    Case 20 to 25
        lblMsg.Text = "Young Adult"
    Case Is > 26
        lblMsg.Text = "Adult"
    Case Else
        lblMsg.Text = "Bad Input"
End Select
```

The select case statement shown considers 6 different ranges of ages and based on the age range outputs a message. The last case is output if the age entered is outside the acceptable range, in this instance it would be triggered by a negative number.

### 7.9.1 Step-by-Step Exercise

Create a new project named GermanCount. This program will allow the user to enter a number 1 to 10 and receive a message giving the number in German. The number will be displayed in a MessageBox.Show method with only the OK button.

Build a form, see example in Figure 7.9.1.1
    TextBox (Name) property txtNum
    Button (Name) property btnGO, Text Property &Go
    Button (Name) property btnExit, Text Property E&xit
    Form (Name) property frmGerman,
        Text Property "German Numbers"

*Figure 7.9.1.1*

85

Once the form is complete create click events for the Exit button and the Go button. See Figure 7.9.1.2 for the partial code for the Go button Click Event. You complete the code using the following information:

| | | |
|---|---|---|
| **6** | **=** | **Sechs** |
| **7** | **=** | **Sieben** |
| **8** | **=** | **Acht** |
| **9** | **=** | **Neun** |
| **10** | **=** | **Zhen** |

Below is the code for numbers 1 through 5:

```
btnGO                                                          Click

    Private Sub btnGO_Click(ByVal sender As System.Object, ByVal e As System.EventArgs) Handles btnGO.Click
        Dim intNum As Integer
        If Integer.TryParse(txtNum.Text, intNum) Then
            Select Case intNum
                Case 1
                    MessageBox.Show("Eins")
                Case 2
                    MessageBox.Show("Zwei")
                Case 3
                    MessageBox.Show("Drei")
                Case 4
                    MessageBox.Show("Vier")
                Case 5
                    MessageBox.Show("Funf")

                Case Else
                    MessageBox.Show("Only Integers from 1 to 10 Accepted")
            End Select
        Else
            MessageBox.Show("Conversion to Integer Failed")
        End If
    End Sub
End Class
```

## Figure 7.9.1.2

Once your code is complete and error free, test all ten options to insure the correct message is shown. Also, test with a number greater than 10 and then enter a letter and make sure the TryParse is also working.

## 7.10 Summary

The decision structure allows the program to make basic choices on comparing values or contants of variables. There are several different commands that make decisions.

Decisions are based on evaluating two operands. The operand may be a literal or a variable. The expression must always evaluate to either True or False. These expressions are referred to as "Boolean Expressons". Comparisons are done using Relaional Operators and Logical Operators.

The If...Then structure is a single sided comparison. An expression is evaluated and if the evaluation is true, a statement or block of statements are executed. If the expression evaluates to False, the program continues with the statement after the True statement or statement block.

The If..Then..Else...Endif is similar, the exception is that you supply one set of code if the expression evaluates to True and a different set for False.

The "IF" statements can be nested. Simply, the True or False code may contain additional IF statements.

When there is a large number of evaluations of a varaible, the Switch statement may be used, usually to replace a nested IF statement structure or a list of IF statements.

# Lesson 8
# Repetition (Looping)

## 8.1  Repetition

The Repetition structure is also known as "Looping", is another valuable tool for the programmer.  It is used to execute a block of code a number of times or until a particular condition exists.  There are a number of types of loops.  Loops fall into two general categories. Some are pretest loops, that is a loop that tests the loop condition before executing any statements.  This means that there is a chance that the loop statements are never executed.

The other category of loops are posttest loops.  These are loops that test the exit condition at the end of the loop.  This type of loop always executes its statements at least once.

Counter controled loops are loops that are executed based on a value in a numeric variable.  For example, the code tells the computer to execute the loop statement ten times.  A counter is set up and the loop tests the counter in the boolean expression and when it reaches the predetermined value, the loop exits.

User controled loops are loops that ask the user if the loop should exit. Each time through the loop statements the user is asked if they wish to continue.  This may be a question asked of the user or the user may enter a value that indicates the desire to end the loop.  (Another situation is when the loop exit is determined by the end of data in a file.)

## 8.2  Do While Loops

The While loop can be a pretest loop or a posttest loop.  As a pretest loop the Boolean Expression is placed before the loop statements and if the boolean expression tests to TRUE, the statements in the loop are executed.  If it tests to FALSE, the processing continues with the first statement after the loop.

As a posttest loop the boolean expression is tested after doing the loop statements once.  If it tests TRUE control passes back to the first statement in the loop.  If it tests FALSE control passes to the next statement after the loop.

PreTest Loop:  (starts when condition is true, ends when condition becomes false)

SYNTAX:

```
Do While boolean expression
     statement(s)
Loop
```

**or**

PostTest Loop: (executes the loop once and continues only while the contition is true)

SYNTAX:

```
Do
     statements
Loop While boolean expression
```

The statements may be an valid Visual Basic statements. The end of the loop statements are indicated by the **Loop** statement.

It is important that there is a statement in the loop that will change the boolean expression so at some point it tests false to exit the loop. A loop that never reaches a condition where the loop can exit is known as an "Infinite Loop". A loop may also be exited by a break statement.

### 8.3  Do Until Loops

The Do loop is a also a pretest or posttest loop. As a pretest loop the Boolean Expression is placed before the loop statements and if the boolean expression tests to FALSE, the statements in the loop are executed. If it tests to TRUE, the processing continues with the first statement after the loop.

As a posttest loop the loop statements are executed once and at the end the Boolean Expression is evaluated. If it tests to FALSE the loop returns to the top at the Do statement and the loop statements are executed again. The Boolean expression is evaluated at the end of the loop statements and if tests to TRUE the next statement after the loop is executed.

PreTest Loop:  (starts when condition is false, ends when condition becomes true)

SYNTAX

```
Do Until boolean expression
     statements
Loop
```

**or**

PostTest Loop: (executes the loop once and continues only while the contition is false)

SYNTAX:

```
Do
     statements
Loop Until boolean expression
```

89

The statements may be an valid Visual Basic statements. The end of the loop statements are indicated by the **Loop** statement.

It is important that there is a statement in the loop that will change the boolean expression so at some point it tests false to exit the loop. A loop that never reaches a condition where the loop can exit is known as an "Infinite Loop". A loop may also be exited by a break statement.

## 8.4   InputBox Function

In a previous chapter we have learned to gather data from Text Boxes. However, when it is necessary to gather a large number of inputs or an unknown number of entries, a text box has its limitations. How many text boxes would be necessary? I can't make a form that big, and other problems arise at design time.

We can solve this by using the InputBox. The input box expands on the MessageBox function, in that it allows the user to input data into control similar to a text box. The InputBox is used when there are a large number of inputs or an unknown number of inputs are reqired.

The InputBox function displays a window to request the user to enter a value. When the user is finished they can select the OK button to transmit the value to the code or the CANCEL button to close the InputBox.

Unlinke the Text box control, the InputBox function returns a string value to the calling statement. The syntax for the InputBox:

```
strValue = InputBox(prompt, title, default)
```

The input box will display a form with a box to enter a value, a prompt to the user stating what is to be entered and two buttons, OK and Cancel. The InputBox function expects at least two strings. The first string is the prompt, a description of what the user is to enter. The second string is the title, a string that is displayed in the blue border at the top left of the InputBox. An optional third string is a default value, that when included, is displayed each time the InputBox is generated and can be replaced with another value. This is used when there is a value that may be entered more often than any other value, or to insure that if the user clicks on the OK button a valid value is returned to the program.

### 8.4.1 Step-by-Step Exercise

We will create a new project named Rainfall. This application gathers rainfall statistics for 12 months and outputs the total and the average for the year. We will accept the monthly rainfall using the InputBox.

After you create the new project called Rainfall, create the form as shown in Figure 8.4.1.1.

Set the (Name) property for Label4 to lblTotal and for Label5 to lblAvg. Name the buttons as follows Enter is btnEnter, Clear is btnClear and Exit is btnExit. The text properties are shown in the buttons in the sample form.

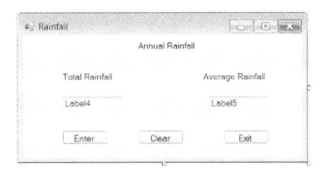

***Figure 8.4.1.1***

The next step is to generate the click event code for each button on the form. The code is shown in Figure 8.4.1.2.

```
Public Class frmRain

    Private Sub btnExit_Click(ByVal sender As System.Object, ByVal e As System.EventArgs) Handles btnExit.Click
        Me.Close()
    End Sub

    Private Sub btnClear_Click(ByVal sender As System.Object, ByVal e As System.EventArgs) Handles btnClear.Click
        lblAvg.Text = " "
        lblTotal.Text = " "
    End Sub

    Private Sub btnEnter_Click(ByVal sender As System.Object, ByVal e As System.EventArgs) Handles btnEnter.Click
        Dim intCount As Integer = 1
        Dim dblRain As Double
        Dim dblTotal As Double
        Dim dblAvg As Double

        dblTotal = 0
        intCount = 1
        Do While intCount < 12
            dblRain = CDbl(InputBox("Enter Monthly Rainfall, Month #: " & intCount))
            dblTotal += dblRain
            intCount += 1
        Loop
        lblTotal.Text = dblTotal.ToString("n")
        dblAvg = dblTotal / 12
        lblAvg.Text = dblAvg.ToString("n")
    End Sub
End Class
```

***Figure 8.4.1.2***

91

Once completed and the program compiles, run the program with some test data.  Make sure the total and average is correct for each set of test data.

## 8.5   ListBox Control

While label controls are useful in displaying information on the form, it is not the best for displaying lists of data.  The control that most fits this application is the ListBox control.  A ListBox control displays a list of items and allows the user to select an item from the list, add or remove items from the list or clear all of the items in the list.

Items can be added to the control or deleted from the control within the code.  The Items.Add method adds items to the ListBox contorl and the contents of the control can be cleared with the Items.Clear method.

SYNTAX:
```
lstBoxName.Items.Add()
```

On a form there is a ListBox named lstGreeting.  Create code to display two lines of strings in the listBox using the Add method. Use the following code:


EXAMPLE:

```
lstGreeting.Items.Add("Hello, World!")
lstGreeting.Items.Add("from Computer Studies")
```


SYNTAX:
```
lstBoxName.Items.Clear()
```

To clear the listBox named lstNumbers use the following code:

EXAMPLE:

```
lstNumbers.Items.Clear()
```

Items may be inserted into a specific location in the list by using the Items.Insert(Index, Item) method.  Index and Item are requir7310.97 ed parameters indicating the location to insert the item and the text for the item to be listed.

Items may be removed in two ways.  Items.Remove(Item) removes by name and Items.RemoveAt(Index) removes the item at a specific location.

92

The term Index used in the methods are sequential numbers that indicate the position of the item in the list. The first item in a list has an index value of zero (0), the second item has an index value of one (1) and so on to the end of the list. This provides two ways to address the contents of the list, by name or by index number.

The Items.Count method lets the program inquire how many items to expect in the list. It will return a value that indicates the number of items in the list.

When it is necessary to allow the user to select an item for processing, the SelectedIndex or SelectedItem methods will return either the index number of the item or the actual value of the item to the progrm.

## 8.6   For Next Loops

A For Next loop allows the program to execute a loop a specified number of times. This is perhaps, the best example and choice for a counter controlled loop. The biggest advantage is that you set up all the conditions in the For statement and you do not have to remember to put in a statement to make sure the loop exits.

SYNTAX:

```
FOR countval = startval TO endval [step increment]
      loop statement(s)
NEXT [countval]
```

The keyword FOR is followed by a variable name that will keep count of the loop iterations. The variable is followed by an operand indicating the start value of the loop counter (an operand can be a variable containing an integer or a integer numeric literal) this is followd by the keyword TO. Next is the operand that indicates the value that will end the loop. Lastly the optional step increment. This is a 1 by default. A negative value will decrement the counter variable.

After this is the loop statement or statements. The end of loop boundary is indicated by the Next statement. There is also the option of putting the name of the counter variable after the Next statement. This serves as documentation especially important when dealing with nested For Next Loops.

Looking at a simple For loop statement. For example, if you needed to execute a code segment 5 times a For loop might look something like this:

```
For intCounter = 1 To 5 Step + 1
      ' code to be repeated goes here'
Next
```

Yes, you could use a while loop to do the same thing but it would look something like this:

```
intCounter = 1
Do While intCounter <=5
    ' code to be repeated goes here'
    ' the following line must be used to avoid'
    ' creating an infinite loop'
    intCounter = intCounter + 1
Loop
```

It appears that the simplest approach is the For Next loop. More compact code and easier to read.

A loop may also be the result of decrementing a counter. To use a For loop to loop on a decrementing counter the following code could be used.

```
For intCounter = 10 To 0 Step - 1
    ' code to be repeated goes here'
Next
```

The optional step argument could also be used to generate a loop giving all of the odd numbers between 1 and 20 by using the following code.:

```
For intCounter = 1 To 20 Step + 2
    ' code to be repeated goes here'
Next
```

For the even numbers, just change the start to the first even number.

```
For intCounter = 2 To 20 Step + 2
    ' code to be repeated goes here'
Next
```

As you can now see, the step can be any integer value required. The step could be by 5, 10, 100 or any valid integer.

### 8.6.1 Step-by-Step Exercise

Create a new project named CountDisplay. Using Figure 8.6.1.1 Do the following:

Place a ListBox control on the form and change the (Name) property to lstDisplay.

Place 3 buttons on the form. Button1, (Name) btnCount, Text= Count; Button2, (Name) btnClear, Text=Clear; Button3, (Name) btnExit, Text=Exit.

*Figure 8.6.1.1*

Next code the click events for the three buttons as shown in Figure 8.6.1.2.

When the code is complete and all errors are eliminated, test the application. Click on the Count button and make sure the numbers 1 thru 10 are displayed in the list box. The clear button should clear all numbers in the list box. I bet you can guess by now what the Exit button will do.

```
Public Class Form1

    Private Sub btnCount_Click(ByVal sender As System.Object, ByVal e As System.EventArgs) Handles btnCount.Click
        Dim intCtr As Integer
        For intCtr = 1 To 10
            lstDisplay.Items.Add(intCtr)
        Next
    End Sub

    Private Sub btnClear_Click(ByVal sender As System.Object, ByVal e As System.EventArgs) Handles btnClear.Click
        lstDisplay.Items.Clear()
    End Sub

    Private Sub btnExit_Click(ByVal sender As System.Object, ByVal e As System.EventArgs) Handles btnExit.Click
        Me.Close()
    End Sub
End Class
```

*Figure 8.6.1.2*

This exercise demonstrates the ListBox Control and the For Next loop.

Now use the step argument to alter your For loop to count up by other values. Change the starting value, the ending value and experiment with other scenarios. Do the odd and even examples.

## *8.7 Nested Loops*

There may be circumstances where loops may be required inside other loops. This is called nesting the loops. A For Next loop may be nested inside another For Next Loop. A Do While loop may be inside a For Next loop or vice versa. Any combination of the various types of loops may be used. You may nest as many loops as required but the more complex your code, the more difficult to test and to maintain.

Our example is the nesting of a For Next loop inside (Inner Loop) a second For Next loop (Outer Loop). The Outer loop will repeat 4 times and the inner loop will execute 2 times each time the outer loop executes.

### 8.7.1 Step-by-Step Exercise

Create a new project named Nested.

Create a form using the example form in Figure 8.7.1.1
Name the ListBox lstDisplay

Name the 3 buttons:
    btnGO
    btnClear
    btnExit

Text properties:
    GO
    Clear
    Exit

**Figure 8.7.1.1**

96

Enter the code for the button click events as shown in Figure 8.7.1.2.

```
Public Class Form1

    Private Sub btnGO_Click(ByVal sender As System.Object, ByVal e As System.EventArgs) Handles btnGO.Click
        Dim intX As Integer
        Dim intY As Integer
        For intX = 1 To 4
            lstDisplay.Items.Add(intX & " Outer")
            For intY = 1 To 2
                lstDisplay.Items.Add("   " & intY & " Inner")
            Next
        Next
        lstDisplay.Items.Add("List Terminated")
    End Sub

    Private Sub btnClear_Click(ByVal sender As System.Object, ByVal e As System.EventArgs) Handles btnClear.Click
        lstDisplay.Items.Clear()
    End Sub

    Private Sub btnExit_Click(ByVal sender As System.Object, ByVal e As System.EventArgs) Handles btnExit.Click
        Me.Close()
    End Sub
End Class
```

### *Figure 8.7.1.2*

When the code is working, test it to insure all three buttons work.

## *8.8   MultiColumn ListBox and Checked List Boxes*

There is also an option to construct a ListBox that contains multiple columns.  There is a property of the ListBox Multicolumn, this property when set to TRUE will allow the listbox to contain multiple columns.

The CheckedListBox Control is a variation of the ListBox.  Properties and methods are the same for both controls.

## *8.9   Summary*

Repetition or "looping" is used to execute a block of code a number of times or until a particular condition exists, like end of file or the user terminating the loop.

Pretest loops like the Do While and For Next loop structures, test the condition for entering the loop BEFORE executing the loop instructions. So, it is possible with a pretest loop that the loop instructions will never be executed.

Posttest loops are loops that test the condition for repetition, AFTER executing the loop instruction.  This means that the loop instructions are executed at least one time.  An example of this type of loop is the DO loops.

The InputBox function expands on the MessageBox function.  It allow the user to enter a value.  This can be useful where there are a large number of inputs or when the exact number of inputs are unknown.

The ListBox control is used to display lists of information on the form and allow the user to select one or more items from the list for input. Items may be added, deleted, and the list may be cleared as the program is running.

The chapter also discussed the use of multicolumn list boxes and checkedlistbox controls as other ways to allow the user to enter data accurately.

# Lesson 9
## Arrays

### 9.1   Arrays

Simply, an array is a group of variables, all with the same name.  Each value stored in an array is called an element.  The elements are accessed by using the array name plus a value that refers to the elements position in the array.  This value is called a subscript or an index.

An array is a variable that can hold several values of the same data type.  The names of the days of the week are all string values.  They are all days of the week and giving them unique names is not the easiest way to refer to them in a program.  In the non computing world we might refer to Sunday as the first day of the week, Monday as the second day of the week and so on though Saturday as the seventh day of the week.

In programming we can use the same concept using arrays to provide the same means of reference to the various days within a program.

### 9.2   Declaring Arrays

Declaring an array is similar to declaring any other variable.  The general syntax is:

```
Dim ArrayName(uppersubscript) As DataType
```

ArrayName is the name of the array.  The uppersubscript is the value of the array's highest subscript.  It is a positive integer, named constant containing a positive integer, or a variable containing a positive integer.  An example of the code:

```
Dim intValu(5) As Integer
```

This statement declares an array of six elements, zero being the first element and 5 being the sixth element.  Note that Arrays are zero based, the first element of an array is element 0.

| Element Value | Element Name |
|:---:|:---:|
| 0 | intValu(0) |
| 0 | intValu(1) |

| Element Value | Element Name |
|---|---|
| 0 | intValu(2) |
| 0 | intValu(3) |
| 0 | intValu(4) |
| 0 | intValu(5) |

Since no values have been assigned to the elements of the array, All elements contain the value of zero (0).
We can also initialize the elements of the array at declaration time as well as add or change values of the elements during program execution. The next example shows an array of 6 names in an array named strName.

```
Dim strName() As String= {"Joe", "Sue", "Sam", "Ike",
"May", "Nat"}
```

| Element Value | Element Name |
|---|---|
| Joe | strName(0) |
| Sue | strName(1) |
| Sam | strName(2) |
| Ike | strName(3) |
| May | strName(4) |
| Nat | strName(5) |

Note: if you initialize the array at declaration you do not provide an uppersubscript value in the declaration.

## 9.2.1 Step-by-Step Exercise

Create a form with a listBox (lstValues) control and a button control (btnGo).  See Figure 9.2.1.1

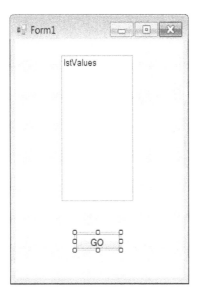

*Figure 9.2.1.1*

Now create the code Code:  Declare an array for 10 values.   Next, create a for loop to take in 10 values  Finally, a for loop to display the 10 values entered in a list box
See Figure 9.2.1.2

```
Form1.vb  ×  Form1.vb [Design]
btnGO                                                              ▼    Click

Public Class Form1

    Private Sub btnGO_Click(sender As System.Object, e As System.EventArgs) Handles btnGO.Click
        Dim intNumbers As Integer
        Dim intArrayNum(10) As Integer

        For intNumbers = 1 To 10
            intArrayNum(intNumbers) = CInt(InputBox("Enter a Number"))
        Next
        For intNumbers = 1 To 10
            lstValues.Items.Add(intArrayNum(intNumbers))
        Next
    End Sub
End Class
```

*Figure 9.2.1.2*

Test the program by entering ten (10) numbers as directed. The numbers will be displayed exactly as entered.

## 9.3  Manipulating Arrays

First lets look at Accessing array elements. We will examine using the For Next loop to write to the contents of a loop and then read from a loop.

```
Dim intX As Integer
Dim decRate(5) As Decimal

decRate(0) = 12.98
decRate(1) = 7.75
decRate(2) = 9.99
decRate(3) = 16.67
decRate(4) = 11.33
decRate(5) = 9.12

For intX = 0 to 5
    lstDisplay.Items.Add("Pay Rate $" & decRate(intX)
Next intX
```

Note that it took 6 statements to load the array and only 3 to display the contents of the array.

We could make this code more useful and compact by asking the user to enter the values in the array. This is where the input box becomes very useful.

```
Dim intX As Integer
Dim decInp As Decimal
Dim decRate(5) As Decimal

For intX = 0 to 5
    decInp = InputBox("Enter Value " & intX)
    lstDisplay.Items.Add(decInp)
Next intX

For intX = 0 to 5
    lstDisplay.Items.Add("Pay Rate $" & decRate(intX)
Next intX
```

More compact and more useful. Now the user can enter any sequence of six values using the InputBox function.

The program can obtain the size of an array by accessing the Length property of the array.  Examine the following code:

```
Dim strName() As String={"Sam", "Joe", "Sue", "Lee"}
Dim intCount As Integer
For intCount = 0 to strName.Length-1
     MessageBox.Show(strNames(intCount))
Next
```

Examine the code and see how the upperbound element of the array is found by accessing the length property.  Since the intCount starts at 0 we need to subtract 1 from the length amount.

### 9.3.1 Step-by-Step Exercise

Create a new project named Sales.

This program will allow the user to enter 12 sales amounts and then display the amounts in a listbox.

Create a form similar to the one shown in Figure 9.3.1.1.

*Figure 9.3.1.1*

Now, enter the code for the click events as shown in Figure 9.3.1.2.

103

```
Public Class Form1

    Private Sub btnGO_Click(ByVal sender As System.Object, ByVal e As System.EventArgs) Handles btnGO.Click
        Dim intCount As Integer
        Dim decSales As Decimal
        Dim decArraySls(8) As Decimal

        For intCount = 0 To decArraySls.Length - 1
            decSales = InputBox("Enter Sales Amount")
            decArraySls(intCount) = decSales
        Next

        For intCount = 0 To decArraySls.Length - 1
            lstDisplay.Items.Add(decArraySls(intCount))
        Next

    End Sub

    Private Sub btnExit_Click(ByVal sender As System.Object, ByVal e As System.EventArgs) Handles btnExit.Click
        Me.Close()
    End Sub
End Class
```

**Figure 9.3.1.2**

When your code is working test to insure the listbox is generated correctly.


## 9.4   Parallel Arrays

An array can hold related data of a single data type.  An example is an array of product names, all string data.  A group of related data (all product names), all of the data type string.  What if we had a group of related data, in an array, all of the data type numeric, and this data had a one to one relationship to our names array?  Using our example, an array of product names and an array of the retail price of each of the products.

| Array #1 Products | Index # | Array #2 Price |
|---|---|---|
| Monitor 17 inch | 0 | 129.99 |
| Monitor 22 inch | 1 | 149.99 |
| Deluxe Tower | 2 | 239.95 |

104

| Array #1<br>Products | Index<br># | Array #2<br>Price |
|---|---|---|
| Premium Tower | 3 | 469.95 |
| Laser Printer | 4 | 299.99 |

This table shows the name of the arrays at the top, (Products and Price). Under each array name are the element values associated with that array. There are the same number of elements in each array. The center column shows the index value used to reference the elements in both arrays. The numbers are 0 to 4 indicating five elements in each array.

This illustrates that Products(2) Deluxe Tower and Price(2) 239.95 are associated as the product name and price of those elements. This also shows that order of elements in the parallel arrays is important.

### 9.4.1 Step-by-Step Exercise

Create a project named School.

Create a form named frmStudents as shown in Figure 9.4.1.

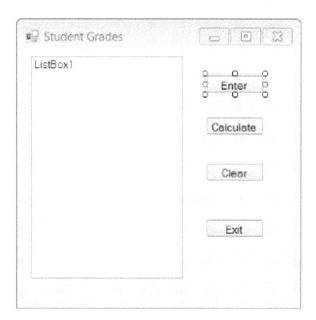

*Figure 9.4.1*

Name the Controls as follows:

| Control | (Name) | Text |
|---------|--------|------|
| Form1 | frmStudent | Student Grades |
| ListBox1 | lstDisplay | |
| Button1 | btnEnter | Enter |
| Button2 | btnCalculate | Calculate |
| Button3 | btnClear | Clear |
| Button4 | btnExit | Exit |

Now create the code for the click event for each button as shown in Figure 9.4.2.

Note that the arrays that hold the student name and grade are placed in the Global area, just below the Public Class line. This makes the arrays available to the clice event for Enter and the click event for Calculate.

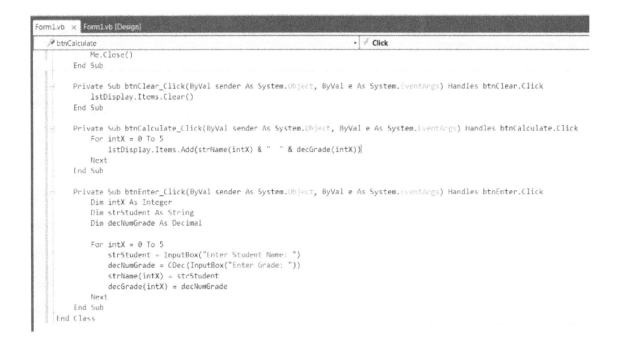

```vb
Form1.vb  ×  Form1.vb [Design]

btnCalculate                                                      ▾   Click

            Me.Close()
        End Sub

        Private Sub btnClear_Click(ByVal sender As System.Object, ByVal e As System.EventArgs) Handles btnClear.Click
            lstDisplay.Items.Clear()
        End Sub

        Private Sub btnCalculate_Click(ByVal sender As System.Object, ByVal e As System.EventArgs) Handles btnCalculate.Click
            For intX = 0 To 5
                lstDisplay.Items.Add(strName(intX) & "   " & decGrade(intX))
            Next
        End Sub

        Private Sub btnEnter_Click(ByVal sender As System.Object, ByVal e As System.EventArgs) Handles btnEnter.Click
            Dim intX As Integer
            Dim strStudent As String
            Dim decNumGrade As Decimal

            For intX = 0 To 5
                strStudent = InputBox("Enter Student Name: ")
                decNumGrade = CDec(InputBox("Enter Grade: "))
                strName(intX) = strStudent
                decGrade(intX) = decNumGrade
            Next
        End Sub
    End Class
```

**Figure 9.4.2**

Once the code has been entered and all syntax error resolved, test the program. Click on the enter button and respond to the Message Boxes with Student Names and Grades. Once you have completed filling the array, click on the calculate button and it should transfer the contents of the parallel arrays to the list box. See Figure 9.4.3.

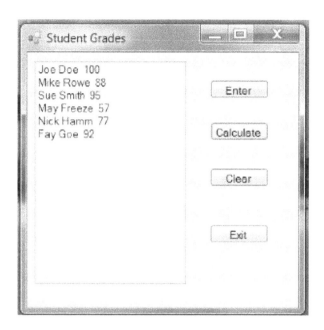

**Figure 9.4.3**

The program should request six names and grades. Then display as shown in the example.

## 9.5  Summary

An array is a group of variables, all with the same name. The elements of an array are differentiated by an index number, (enclosed in parenthesis), appended to the arrayname. The first element of the array is arrayname(0), the second element is arrayname(1) and so on. Zero is always the first element of an array.

Arrays may be initialized when declared, or empty arrays filled by code statements. Elements may be added, deleted, modified as the program runs. The size of the array is determined when the array is declared.

Parallel arrays are groups of arrays about a common subject. An Employee Group might consist of a Name Array, A Date of Hire Array, A Pay Rate Array, and A Department Array. Each employee would have an entry in each array at the same index number in each array.

## Unit Four – Working With Data

Lesson 10 – Menus

Lesson 11 – Multiple Forms

Lesson 12 - Procedures and Functions

# Lesson 10
## Menus

### 10.1 Menus Overview

Most of the applications we deal with on a daily basis have some type of menuing system to allow us to make choices in our processing. In a Word Processor we have choices that allow us to save files, print files, change the font type and size, italicize, bold, underscore and on and on. Many applications have large numbers of choices. So many that it would be impossible to represent them all on one form. So, the logical solution is a menuing system.

In example Figure 10.1.1 the menu for OpenOffice Writer is shown. It is fairly representative of applications using a menuing system. Left to right File (File Operations), Edit (Editing operations for the current open file), etc. This menu has 9 choices at the top line

**Figure 10.1.1**

The next Figure 10.1.2 shows the choices under the top level menu item labeled File. The four items marked show some of the more popular choices when working with the file. Create a New File, Save the existing file, Print the current file, and exit the Application.

**Figure 10.1.2**

109

Examine the choices in the menu and you will see that each of them involve a File based operation. This is the hierarchy of the organization of menus. The top level choice Edit will contain items that relate to the editing of the current document in the work area.

### 10.2 Creating Menus with the Menu Editor

Menus are such an important part of applications that Microsoft has included a Menu control that assists the programmer in creating menus easily.

Before beginning menu creation, it is a good idea to plan out your menu carefully. Group your choices logically and then it is always a good idea to put them in the order of the most used at the top and least used at the bottom.

In Figure 10.2.1 we see the Toolbar for Visual Basic with the control to start menu creation (MenuStrip) circled.

**Figure 10.2.1**

To start menu creation, double click on the MenuStrip selection and it will place the entry point for your first menu item on your form.

In Figure 10.2.2, the menu creation has started. Note the way the MenuStrip control leads through the placement of the menu items. Top level, then sub level with further choices for sub-sub levels.

In the example the top level choice File has been placed with a sub level of Exit below. Also note that the control has provided placeholders for the next top level menu item, the next first sub level menu item, and the sub-sub level item placeholder for the first sublevel menu item. If nothing is typed the menu item is not created. Don't forget each of these menu items can have sub menu items.

110

While there does not seem to be a limit in sub menus, I recommend that you only go to one level of sub menus. If more than that is required, consider an additional top level menu item.

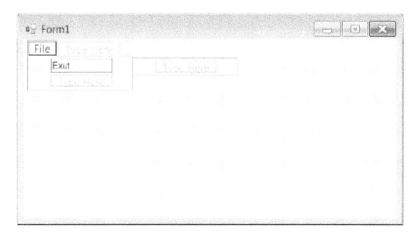

*Figure 10.2.2*

The Figure 10.2.3 shows a completed selection list for the main menu item named "File". There are no sub menus show in this illustration. Each of these choices will be a clickable event, just like a button click event.

*Figure 10.2.3*

The Figure 10.2.4 shows the next menu item "Edit" completed selection list that shows items that have sub menus.

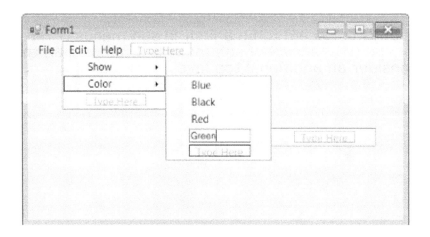

**Figure 10.2.4**

Note the items under "Edit" have arrows to their right.  These arrows indicate sub menu items exist.  For the "Color" selection there are four sub menu items, each will be a "clickable event".

The "clickable events" we have been discussing are events coded just like we coded the button_click events.

### 10.3 Naming Menu Items

Like everthing else in VB programming, naming these "clickable events" is very important.  Each of the top menu items need names to indicate their poisition in the hierarchy.  Then the items in the selection list need to be clearly identified as well as some indication as to which top level menu they belong to.

| File | | Edit | | Help |
|------|------|------|------|------|
| mnuFile | | mnuEdit | | mnuHelp |
| | mnuFileNew | | mnuEditShow | mnuShowVisible | |
| | mnuFileOpen | | | mnuShowInvisible | |
| | mnuFileSave | | mnuEditColor | mnuEditColorBlue | |
| | mnuFileSaveAs | | | mnuEditColorBlack | |

| File | | | Edit | Help |
|------|---|---|------|------|
| mnuFilePrint | | | mnuEditColorRed | |
| mnuFileExit | | | mnuEditColorGreen | |

As you can see in the table above, every selection name begins with "mnu". This clearly identifies the click event belongs to a menu item.

## 10.4 Coding Menu Items

Now we can double click on a menu item and generate the associated click events.

```
Public Class frmMenu

    Private Sub mnuFileExit_Click(ByVal sender As System.Object, ByVal e As System.EventArgs) Handles mnuFileExit.Click
        Me.Close()
    End Sub

    Private Sub mnuEditColorBlue_Click(ByVal sender As Object, ByVal e As System.EventArgs) Handles mnuEditColorBlue.Click
        Me.BackColor = Color.Blue
    End Sub

    Private Sub mnuEditColorBlack_Click(ByVal sender As Object, ByVal e As System.EventArgs) Handles mnuEditColorBlack.Click
        Me.BackColor = Color.Black
    End Sub

    Private Sub mnuEditColorRed_Click(ByVal sender As Object, ByVal e As System.EventArgs) Handles mnuEditColorRed.Click
        Me.BackColor = Color.Red
    End Sub

    Private Sub mnuHelp_Click(ByVal sender As Object, ByVal e As System.EventArgs) Handles mnuHelp.Click
        lblMsg.Text = "This is a Menu Demo Program"
    End Sub
End Class
```

### Figure 10.4.1

Figure 10.3.1 shows some of the click events for the menu items in this application. Note the "Me." prefix on many of the commands. This indicates that the form is being referenced. So in this example the Me. Is the equivalent to frmMenu. for all the commands.

These events are coded just as you would code a button click event. All valid code statements may be used in these events.

## 10.5 Check Marks in Menus

Some programs place check marks next to selected items. In our example where the sub menu Color has four different prices, a good practice would be to place a check mark next to the current selected color. In Figure 10.5.1 we see the background is Blue and the selected

113

menu item has been checked. When another color is selected, the check marks are cleared and the appropriate selection gets a check mark. The code for this is noted in Figure 10.6.2.

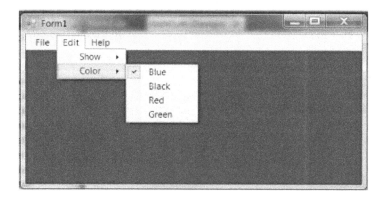

*Figure 10.5.1*

The Figure 10.5.2 shows the same form with the Color Red selected.

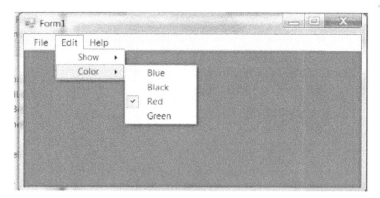

*Figure 10.5.2*

Now, lets examine the code to switch the check marks as the items are selected. This is shown in Figure 10.5.3. The code to set and unset check marks is reflected in the following code:

```
Private Sub mnuEditColorBlue_Click(ByVal sender As Object, ByVal e As System.EventArgs) Handles mnuEditColorBlue.Click
    Me.BackColor = Color.Blue
    mnuEditColorBlue.Checked = True
    mnuEditColorBlack.Checked = False
    mnuEditColorRed.Checked = False
    mnuEditColorGreen.Checked = False
End Sub

Private Sub mnuEditColorBlack_Click(ByVal sender As Object, ByVal e As System.EventArgs) Handles mnuEditColorBlack.Click
    Me.BackColor = Color.Black
    mnuEditColorBlue.Checked = False
    mnuEditColorBlack.Checked = True
    mnuEditColorRed.Checked = False
    mnuEditColorGreen.Checked = False
End Sub

Private Sub mnuEditColorRed_Click(ByVal sender As Object, ByVal e As System.EventArgs) Handles mnuEditColorRed.Click
    Me.BackColor = Color.Red
    mnuEditColorBlue.Checked = False
    mnuEditColorBlack.Checked = False
    mnuEditColorRed.Checked = True
    mnuEditColorGreen.Checked = False
End Sub

Private Sub mnuHelp_Click(ByVal sender As Object, ByVal e As System.EventArgs) Handles mnuHelp.Click
    lblMsg.Text = "This is a Menu Demo Program"
End Sub
```

## Figure 10.5.3

Each click event needs to have the code to unset all the check marks and then set the appropriate check mark for the selection.

## 10.6 Separator Bars in Menus

Separator bars are used to mark off sections of a drop down menu. The purpose is to group selections into logical groupings. In our File instance we want to group start up selections (New, Open); Save selections (Save, SaveAs); Print selections (Print); and Ending selections (Exit).

If you look carefully at the menu selections in any application with drop down menus, you will see the liberal use of these separators. Just look at Visual Basic next time you fire it up.

To add a Separator Bar you need to select the option AFTER the position you wish to place the bar. Then RIGHT CLICK on that selection to open a pop up menu. On that pop up menu there is a choice "Insert" followed by a right arrow. Click on Insert to open the sub menu and on that menu select "Separator". This will place the Separator Bar directly above the selected item.

If you should accidently put the bar in the wrong location you can drag-and-drop the bar into the proper location.

In Figure 10.6.1 examine the following choices:

1.    Right Click on the selection just below where you wish to place the line.
2.    In the popup menu select Insert.
3.    In the next menu select Separator and the bar will be added just above the selection.


Best way to get some better understanding is to practice the menu creation process in Visual Basic.

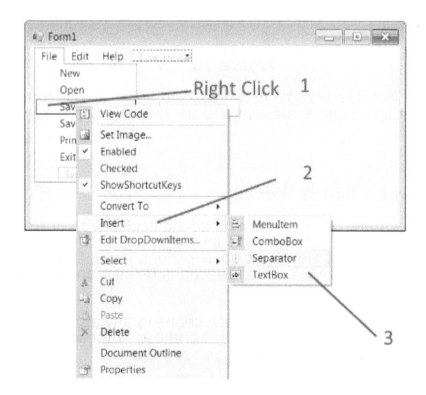

*Figure 10.6.1*


Now, look at Figure 10.6.2 and see the results of a menu with added Separator Bars.

116

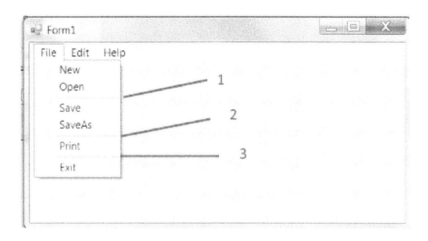

*Figure 10.6.2*

Bar labeled 1 is after New and Open. Bar labeled 2 is after Save and SaveAs. Bar labeled 3 separates Print and Exit.

## 10.7 Random Numbers

Random numbers are supported in Visual Basic.NET. They are easy to implement and can be used in any application where they would be needed.

Syntax of the Rnd() function to create an integer between two numbers. Upperbound is the largest integer and lowerbound is the lowest integer value.

SYNTAX:

```
intVariable = Cint(Int((upperbound * Rnd()) + lowerbound ))
```

### 10.7.1 Step-By-Step Exercise

This application will simulate the rolling of two dice. Click on the ROLL button and two random values appear in the labels. Start a new project named Dice and create the following form:

117

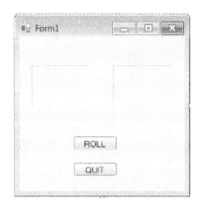

*Figure 10.7.1*

Change the control properties as follows:

| Control | Property | Value |
|---|---|---|
| Label1 | (Name) | lblDie1 |
| | Font | 36   Bold |
| | AutoSize | FALSE |
| | BorderStyle | Fixed3D |
| Label2 | (Name) | lblDie2 |
| | Font | 36  Bold |
| | AutoSize | FALSE |
| | BorderStyle | Fixed3D |
| Button1 | (Name) | btnRoll |
| | Text | ROLL |
| Button2 | (Name) | btnQuit |
| | Text | QUIT |

Then enter the code in Figure 10.7.2:

```
Private Sub btnRoll_Click(ByVal sender As System.Object, ByVal e As System.EventArgs) Handles btnRoll.Click
    Dim intDie1 As Integer
    Dim intDie2 As Integer

    intDie1 = CInt(Int((6 * Rnd()) + 1))
    intDie2 = CInt(Int((6 * Rnd()) + 1))

    lblDie1.Text = intDie1
    lblDie2.Text = intDie2
End Sub

Private Sub btrQuit_Click(ByVal sender As System.Object, ByVal e As System.EventArgs) Handles btnQuit.Click
    Me.Close()
End Sub
End Class
```

**Figure 10.7.2**

Now run the application and click on the ROLL button several times and see the random numbers generated.

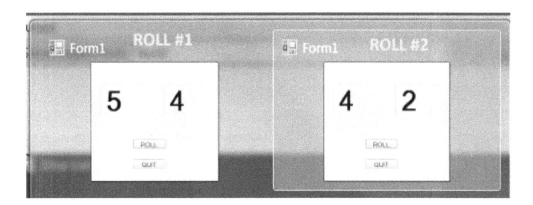

**Figure 10.7.3**

There are six possible values for the sides of a Die.  By using 6 as the upperbound and 1 as the lowerbound, those will be the only integers generated.

## 10.8 Summary

Menus allow the form to have many different choices without the clutter of buttons.  Many applications use menus to give the user multiple choices when running an application.  We are all familiar with the menu order of: File; Edit; View; ….. Help that are on top of many of the application forms we use every day.  Menus have become a standard and probably used in Windows Applications more than buttons.

Random numbers are important to applications like games.  Visual Basic supports a Rnd() function that allows the generation of random numbers.  The statement includes a lowerbound and upperbound numbers so the programmer can define a range of random numbers.

# Lesson 11
## Multiple Forms

### 11.1 Creating Multiple Forms

Up to this point we have only dealt with single form applications. This lesson will explain how to create projects with multiple forms. Multiple forms include popup directions, splash screens as well as multiple processing screens.

To illustrate multiple forms in an application we will create an application with a Help Screen and an about screen, in a Step-By-Step exercise.

### 11.1.1 Step-By-Step Exercise

First we will create a simple applicaton using our new expertise in menus. The application will turn the background color of the form 4 different colors from menu selections. Then on the Help menu two choices. One choice to output a help menu describing how to use the application and a second screen that tells the purpose of the application.

Create a project named **Multiple** and compose a menu system that looks like Figure 11.1.1, Figure 11.1.2, and Figure 11.1.3. Name the Form **frmMain**.

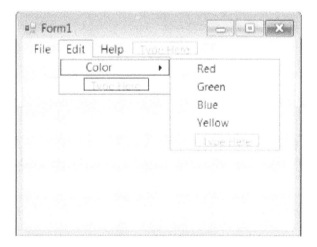

***Figure 11.1.1***

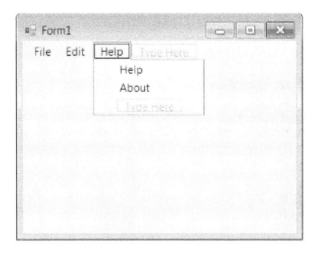

*Figure 11.1.2*

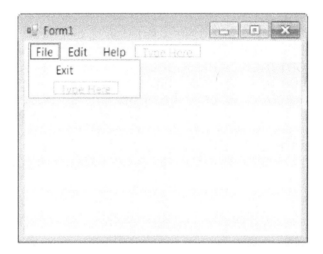

*Figure 11.1.3*

Find the **Project** menu at the top of Visual Basic and select **Add Windows Form** to get the Add New Item dialog box.

Select **Windows Form** from the Templates section of the dialog box. Change the text in the Name text box to **frmHelp.vb** and click on the **Add** button.

Change the text property of the new form to **Help for Multiple**.

On the new form place a button named **btnOK** with the text property set to OK.

Place a text box named **txtComments** with the MultiLine property set to **True** and the WordWrap property set to **True**. Change the Text property to the text shown in Figure 11.1.4. *Hint: click on the arrow to the right of the text area when selected and you will get a larger area to enter your text.*

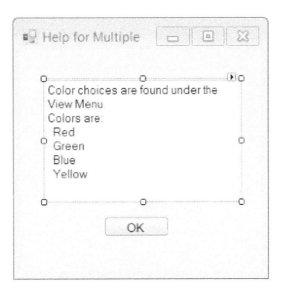

**Figure 11.1.4**

Create another Windows Form named **frmAbout.vb** exactly like the Help Window you just created. The difference is the name of the form (**frmAbout**), the Text property of the form (**About Multiple**) and the Text property of the text box (**This program will display four different color backgrounds on the form. This program was created by *yourname goes here.***) See Figure 11.1.5

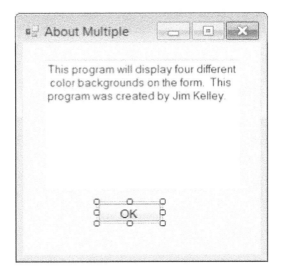

**Figure 11.1.5**

123

Double click on the **OK** button and place *Me.Close()* in the click event generated.

Go to the menu item for About on the main page and double click to generate the click event and program the click event as shown in the code in Figure 11.1.6

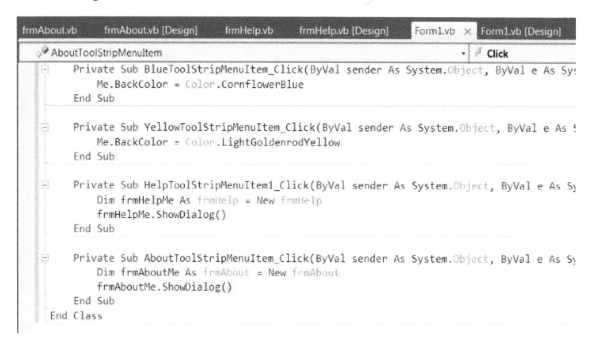

**Figure 11.1.6**

Test your application and make sure everything works. Keep this application as we will be adding a splash screen in Lesson 11.3.

### 11.2  Modal / Modeless Forms

A Modal Form is a form that needs to be closed before you can continue working with the rest of the application. All dialog boxes and MessageBoxes are modal forms.

In the example Figure 11.1.6 the code is building a Modal form. The syntax for a Modal form is:

```
frmAboutMe.ShowDialog()
```

Modeless Forms are forms that do not need to be closed before continuing with application processing.

The syntax for a Modeless Form is

```
formname.Show()
```

Statements after this line will be executed leaving the form open.

### 11.2.1 Step-By-Step Exercise

Create a new application named **Modal** and name the form **frmMain** and the text property **Modal / Modeless**. Place one ListBox control and 4 buttons on the form.The form should look similar to Figure 11.2.1.

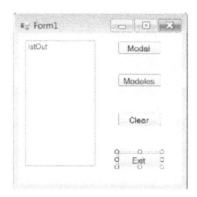

**Figure 11.2.1**

The ListBox should be named **lstOut**. The buttons should be named as follows:

| Control | Property | Value |
|---|---|---|
| Button 1 | (Name) | btnModal |
| | Text | Modal |
| Button 2 | (Name) | btnModeless |
| | Text | Modeless |
| Button 3 | (Name) | btnClear |
| | Text | Clear |
| Button 4 | (Name) | btnExit |
| | Text | Exit |

Next, create a second form named **frmMessage**.  Use the procedure you learned in Lesson 11.1.  Your form should look similar to the one shown in Figure 11.2.2.

*Figure 11.2.2*

Now, enter the code shown in Figure 11.2.3.

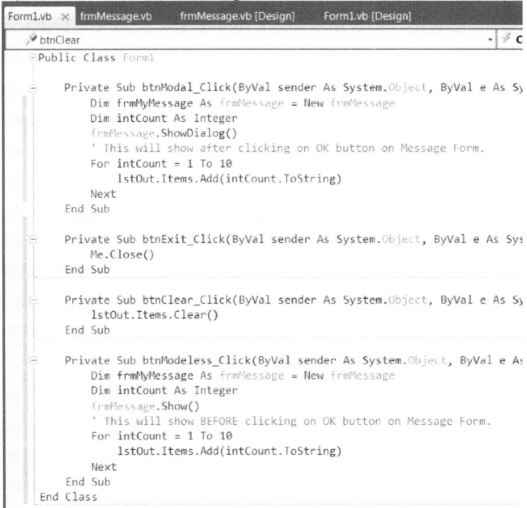

*Figure 11.2.3*

Test your new application.  What happens when you click on the Modal button?  What happens when you click on the Modeless button.  Be sure to clear the ListBox between tests.


### 11.3 Splash Screens

A Splash Screen is just a window that appears briefly when a program first starts.  It usually indicates the name of the program, some copyright information and the version.  Splash screens are just information and appear and disappear by themselves.  Usually there is no title bar and no border and the splash screen appears in the center of the screen.
We will use the program Multiple created in the Lesson 11.1.

Open the **Multiple** Project in Visual Basic and add another form, naming it frmSplash.  Change the form property *FormBorderStyle* to **None**, *StartPosition* property to **CenterScreen**.  Give the form a Background color of a light Yellow.  Place two labels on the screen and change their text properties as shown in Figure 11.3.1.

**Figure 11.3.1**

To make the Splash Form show on the screen at start up time and then remain on the screen for a few seconds before disapearing to allow the Main form to display, we need to put some code in a code module.

Code modules are programs that can be called by any part of the project to perform some task.  To create a code module click on the **Project** menu and select **Add New Item**.


A dialog box will appear, See Figure 11.3.2.

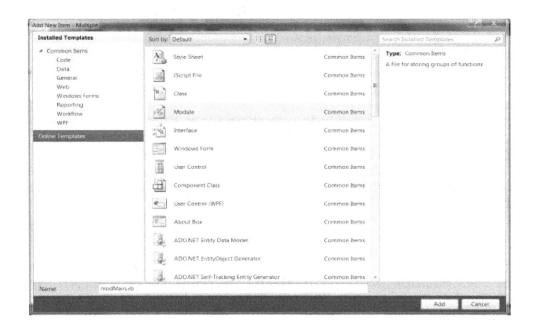

*Figure 11.3.2*

In the dialog box select **Module** and rename the form **modMain.vb** and click on the **Add** button. This will open a code window for the modMain module. Enter the code as shown in Figure 11.3.3.

```
Module modMain
    Dim frmMySplash As frmSplash = New frmSplash
    Dim frmMyMain As frmMultiple = New frmMultiple
    Sub main()
        ' Display the Splash Screen as a Modeless Form
        frmSplash.Show()
        Application.DoEvents()
        'Wait
        Threading.Thread.Sleep(1000)
        'Close the Splash Screen
        frmSplash.Close()
        'Load the Main Form
        frmMyMain.ShowDialog()
    End Sub
End Module
```

*Figure 11.3.3*

Note the code statement after the 'Wait comment:

```
Threading.Thread.Sleep(1000)
```

This causes the program to halt for the number of ticks of the internal clock, indicated in the parenthesis.  The time will be dependent on the internal clock speed of the processor.

Now we need to tell Visual Studio to startup using a Splash Screen.  To do this, go to the Solution Explorer Pane and select the Project Multiple.  Then go to the View Menu and select Property Pages.  This will display a dialog box.  See Figure 11.3.4.

Check the following:

Enable Application Framework must be selected.

Startup Form should be frmMultiple

On the bottom line of the form there is a selection box for Splash Screen.  Select frmSplash.

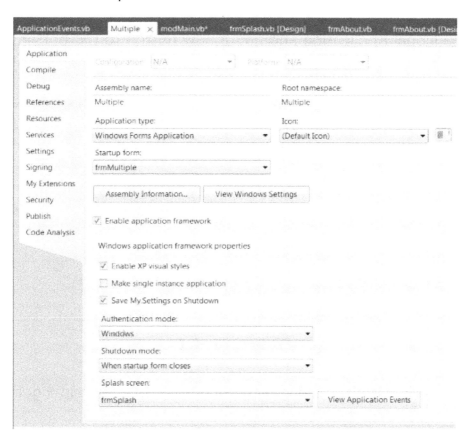

*Figure 11.3.4*

Now you are ready to test the application. When the appliation starts the Splash Screen should show for about 1 second and then disappear. If you want the dialog box to show a longer time change the modMain code. Change the value in the code statement.

```
Threading.Thread.Sleep(2000)
```

Changing 1000 to 2000 will double the time the Splash Screen is visible.


## 11.4   Changing Forms from code at run time.

We can change contents of forms in the code of the forms calling the new form. We will change the Modal application to call a form with directions. We will use the frmMessage to display directions. To do this we will have to change the text property of the label on the form. Yes, we can use the same form several different ways. So, when building forms for multiple form applications, it is important to reuse as many of the forms as possible. This cuts down on programming time as well as load time for loading the application.

Start the Modal Application and add a new button to the bottom of the form. See Figure 11.4.1

*Figure 11.4.1*

Code the click event for the Directions button as shown in Figure 11.4.2

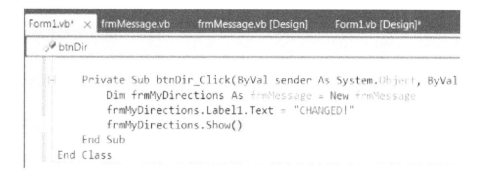

```
Form1.vb*  ×  frmMessage.vb    frmMessage.vb [Design]    Form1.vb [Design]*

  btnDir

       Private Sub btnDir_Click(ByVal sender As System.Object, ByVal
           Dim frmMyDirections As frmMessage = New frmMessage
           frmMyDirections.Label1.Text = "CHANGED!"
           frmMyDirections.Show()
       End Sub
  End Class
```

*Figure 11.4.2*

Now run the program and click on the Directions Button. Then click on the Modal button. Same form...different Message.

By properly planning your multiple forms, you can save programming, program size, program load time by designing some 'All Purpose' forms.

## 11.5   Anchoring and Docking Controls on a Form

**Anchoring** a control is when you set the Anchor property of a control to insure the control maintains its distance from the edge of the parent control to which it is bound and determines how the control is resized with its parent control.

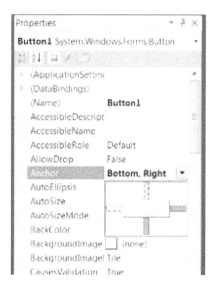

*Figure 11.5.1*

131

Use the control to select the bottom right of the form. To change, click on the bars that extend from the middle of each side of the button. When the bar is dark, it is selected.

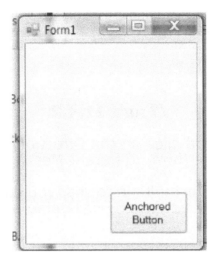

**Figure 11.5.2**

When the application is run, the button appears at the bottom right as shown in Figure 11.5.2.

If the size of the form is changed, stretched horizontally (Figure 11.5.3) or stretched vertically (Figure 11.5.4). The button stays in the same relative position.

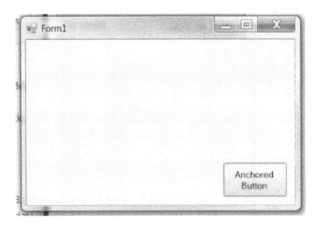

**Figure 11.5.3**
**Form Stretched Horizontally**

*Figure 11.5.4*
*Form Stretched Vertically*

Docking a control resizes a control within its parent control.

Use the control to select the bottom right of the form. To change, click on the bars that extend from the middle of each side of the button. When the bar is dark, it is selected.

*Figure 11.5.5*

133

**Figure 11.5.6**

Figure 11.5.6 shows the form with the button docked at the bottom of the form as indicated in the Dock property.

**Figure 11.5.7**

Figure 11.5.7 shows the form stretched horizontally and the docked button retains it postion across the entire bottom of the form.

## 11.6   Summary

This lesson introduced the concept of multiple forms.  All applications will not always fit on one form.  Multiple forms demonstrate the need to name each form with a descriptive name.

Forms may be modal or modeless.  Modal forms need to be closed before the application continues.  Modeless forms do not suspend the code execution.  A modeless form will remain on the screen and the application code will continue to execute.

# Lesson 12
## Procedures and Functions

In large systems of programs there are tasks that are done in several different parts of the system. Rather than rewrite those tasks each time they are needed, we create procedures or functions. Then each time they are needed the programmer can just call that procedure or fucntion and use written and tested code.

Collectively, Procedures and Functions are referred to as methods in the Object-Oriented world.

This lesson addresses writing general purpose procedures and functions (methods). They are not written to respond to events. These procedures and functions are designed to be called by other statements to do a task.

### 12.1 Procedures

A procedure is called to do a task and when the task is complete, returns control to the instruction after the one that called the procedure. A group of instructions or statements that perform a specific task. A general purpose procedure perform a specifc task and is not triggered by an event. They are called from statements in another procedure.

You have already been working with procedures as you have been creating Event Handlers, and they are procedures.

### 12.1.1 Step-by-Step Exercise

Create a new project and name the project **ProcedureExample**. Figure 12.1.1 shows a form, create a form looking like this form, a listbox and 3 buttons.

*Figure 12.1.1*

Name the controls as follows:

| Control | Property | Value |
| --- | --- | --- |
| Form1 | (Name) | frmDemo |
|  | Text | Procedure Demo. |
| ListBox | (Name) | lstDemo |
|  | Text | Demo |
| Button1 | (Name) | btnGO |
|  | Text | &GO |
| Button2 | (Name) | btnClear |
|  | Text | &Clear |
| Button3 | (Name) | btnExit |
|  | Text | E&xit |

Now we will create a procedure to place a message in the ListBox on our form.

Click on the View Menu item then select code. (See Figure 12.1.2)

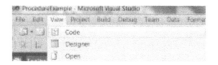

**Figure 12.1.2**

The declaration for a procedure is as follows:

```
Sub procedurename(arguments)
    statements
End Sub
```

Now enter the code for the procedure as shown in Figure 12.1.3.

```
frmDemo                                                    ▾
Public Class frmDemo
    Sub DemoMsg()
        ' This procedures displays a message in a listbox named lstDemo
        lstDemo.Items.Add("")
        lstDemo.Items.Add("This Message is from Procedure DemoMsg()")
        lstDemo.Items.Add("")
    End Sub
End Class
```

*Figure 12.1.3*

If you run the program now, there is no way to make the procedure run. It needs to be called from some other event. Our demo code will call the frmDemo() procedure from the btnGO_Click event. Enter the code in Figure 12.1.4 in the Event Handlers as shown.

```
Public Class frmDemo
    Sub DemoMsg()
        ' This procedures displays a message in a listbox named lstDemo
        lstDemo.Items.Add("")
        lstDemo.Items.Add("This Message is from Procedure DemoMsg()")
        lstDemo.Items.Add("")
    End Sub

    Private Sub btnGO_Click(ByVal sender As System.Object, ByVal e As System.EventArgs) Handles btnGO.Click
        ' Display first message from the btnGO_Click Event
        lstDemo.Items.Add("This is a message line from the btnGO_Click Event")
        'Call the Procedure DemoMsg()
        DemoMsg()
        ' Display last message from the btnGO_Click Event
        lstDemo.Items.Add("This is a message line from the btnGO_Click Event")
    End Sub

    Private Sub btnClear_Click(ByVal sender As System.Object, ByVal e As System.EventArgs) Handles btnClear.Click
        lstDemo.Items.Clear()
    End Sub

    Private Sub btnExit_Click(ByVal sender As System.Object, ByVal e As System.EventArgs) Handles btnExit.Click
        Me.Close()
    End Sub
End Class
```

*Figure 12.1.4*

137

Now test the program. If everything is correct your output should look like Figure 12.1.5.

*Figure 12.1.5*

Examine your output carefully and make sure you understand why the lines were output in the order shown.

## 12.2 *ByVal and ByRef*

There are two ways to pass paramaters (AKA arguments) to procedures and functions. First way is to pass a copy of a variable (Pass ByVal) to the procedure or function. This way the procedure or function works with a COPY of the value and the original value in the calling program is never changed.

The ProcedureExample Project did not pass any information to the procedure because it was not needed to produce the output. Let's open the project and make a few changes to the program.

### 12.2.1 Step-By-Step Exercise

Open the Procedure Example Project and make the following changes to the code. The 10 changes in code are shown in Figure 12.2.1.

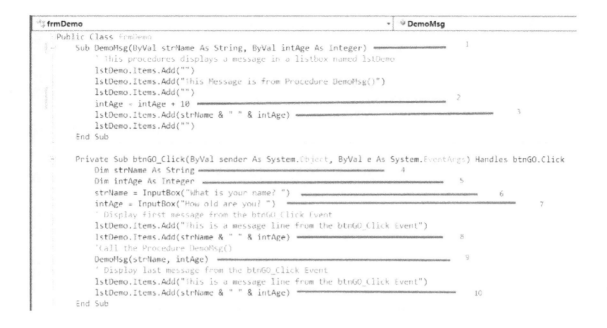

```
frmDemo                                                          DemoMsg
Public Class frmDemo
    Sub DemoMsg(ByVal strName As String, ByVal intAge As Integer) ———— 1
        ' This procedures displays a message in a listbox named lstDemo
        lstDemo.Items.Add("")
        lstDemo.Items.Add("This Message is from Procedure DemoMsg()")
        lstDemo.Items.Add("")
        intAge = intAge + 10 ———— 2
        lstDemo.Items.Add(strName & " " & intAge) ———— 3
        lstDemo.Items.Add("")
    End Sub

    Private Sub btnGO_Click(ByVal sender As System.Object, ByVal e As System.EventArgs) Handles btnGO.Click
        Dim strName As String ———— 4
        Dim intAge As Integer ———— 5
        strName = InputBox("What is your name? ") ———— 6
        intAge = InputBox("How old are you? ") ———— 7
        ' Display first message from the btnGO_Click Event
        lstDemo.Items.Add("This is a message line from the btnGO_Click Event")
        lstDemo.Items.Add(strName & " " & intAge) ———— 8
        'Call the Procedure DemoMsg()
        DemoMsg(strName, intAge) ———— 9
        ' Display last message from the btnGO_Click Event
        lstDemo.Items.Add("This is a message line from the btnGO_Click Event")
        lstDemo.Items.Add(strName & " " & intAge) ———— 10
    End Sub
```

***Figure 12.2.1***

Test your program. If all is correct it should look like Figure 12.2.2.

***Figure 12.2.2***

Note that the contents of variables are consistent in all three outputs. Now add the following statement to the code section before the code line marked 2 in the DemoMsg() Procedure.

```
intAge = intAge + 10
```

Then rerun the program and note the differences. See Figure 12.2.3.

*Figure 12.2.3*

Note the difference in the age shown in the lines printed by the procedure. This is due to the instruction we added that added 10 to the age entered, stored in the variable intAge, passed ByVal to the procedure and stored in the variable intAge in the procedure.

However, after returning to the btnGO_Click event, the value is printed but not changed from the original value. That is due to the passing of a copy of the variable to the procedure. ByVal passes a copy of the contents of the variable and protects the value in the original variable.

The second way is to pass a pointer to the variable being passed (Pass ByREF) so the called procedure or function can use and change the value in the variable in the calling program. To illustrate this we will use a new project similar to the one we used to demonstrate the ByVal choice.

## 12.2.2 Step-By-Step Exercise

Create a project named ByRefExample. The form should be similar to the one shown in Figure 12.2.2.1.

*Figure 12.2.2.1*

140

Name the controls as shown in the table below:

| Control | Property | Value |
| --- | --- | --- |
| Form1 | (Name) | frmDemo |
|  | Text | Function Demo. |
| ListBox | (Name) | lstDemo |
|  | Text | Demo |
| Button1 | (Name) | btnGO |
|  | Text | &GO |
| Button2 | (Name) | btnClear |
|  | Text | &Clear |
| Button3 | (Name) | btnExit |
|  | Text | E&xit |

Now enter the code as shown in Figure 12.2.2.2.

```
Form1.vb  ×  Form1.vb [Design]

btnGO                                                                    ▼   Click

Public Class frmDemo
    Sub DemoMsg(ByVal intNbr1 As Integer, ByRef intNbr2 As Integer)
        ' This procedures displays a message in a listbox named lstDemo
        lstDemo.Items.Add("")
        lstDemo.Items.Add("This Message is from the Function DemoMsg()")
        intNbr1 += 10
        intNbr2 += 10
        lstDemo.Items.Add("First Number:  " & intNbr1 & " ByVal")
        lstDemo.Items.Add("Second Number: " & intNbr2 & " ByRef")
        lstDemo.Items.Add("")
    End Sub

    Private Sub btnGO_Click(ByVal sender As System.Object, ByVal e As System.EventArgs) Handles btnGO.Click
        Dim intNumber1 As Integer
        Dim intNumber2 As Integer
        intNumber1 = InputBox("Enter a number to pass by Value")
        intNumber2 = InputBox("Enter a number to pass by Reference")
        ' Display first message from the btnGO_Click Event
        lstDemo.Items.Add("This is a message line from the btnGO_Click Event")
        lstDemo.Items.Add("Pass " & intNumber1 & " ByVal")
        lstDemo.Items.Add("Pass " & intNumber2 & " ByRef")
        'Call the Procedure DemoMsg()
        DemoMsg(intNumber1, intNumber2)
        ' Display last message from the btnGO_Click Event
        lstDemo.Items.Add("This is a message line from the btnGO_Click Event")
        lstDemo.Items.Add("On return First Number is: " & intNumber1 & " ByVal")
        lstDemo.Items.Add("On return Second Number is: " & intNumber2 & " ByRef")
    End Sub
End Sub
```

### *Figure 12.2.2.2*

When finished, test the program.  You should see output similar shown in Figure 12.2.2.3.

### *Figure 12.2.2.3*

Note the values at all three levels.  Note the difference between values after the procedure has been run.  This demonstrates the important differences between passing argumets ByVal and passing arguments ByRef.

142

## 12.3 Functions

A function is similar to a procdure except for the fact that a function returns a value. The function is called, does the task, but unlike the procedure, it returns a value to the instruction that called the function. Therefore the programmer needs to either store the value returned, use the value returned in an arithmetic expression or display the returned value.

You have been using many built-in functions prior to this lesson. The CInt, IsNumeric(), and many others have been used.

Declaring a function is similar to declaring a procedure:

```
Function functionName (arguments) As DataType
      statements
End Function
```

Calling a function is also different from calling a procedure. Assume three variables have been declared: intNum1, intNum2, and intNum3. Our function called sumIt will add the values in intNum1 and intNum2 returning the sum to be stored in intNum3. The function call to the function would look like this:

```
intNum3 = sumIt(intNum1, intNum2)
```

Now, we will demonstrate a function in the next step-by-step exercise.

### 12.3.1 Step-By-Step Exercise

Create a new project named FunctionExample and create a form that looks like the form in Figure 12.3.1.1.

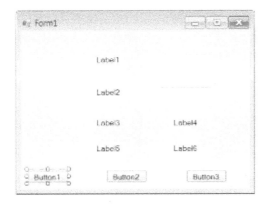

### Figure 12.3.1.1

Name the control objects as shown in the table below.

| Control | Properties | Value |
| --- | --- | --- |
| Form1 | (Name) | frmDemo |
| | Text | Function Demo |
| Label1 | Text | Cost of Meal |
| Label2 | Text | Percent Tip as a decimal |
| Label3 | Text | Amount of Tip: |
| Label5 | Text | Amount of Tax: |
| Label4 | (Name) | lblTip |
| | AutoSize | FALSE |
| | BorderStyle | Fixed3D |
| | Text | |
| | Visible | FALSE |
| Label6 | (Name) | LblTax |
| | AutoSize | FALSE |
| | BorderStyle | Fixed3D |
| | Text | |
| | Visible | FALSE |
| Button1 | (Name) | btnGO |
| | Text | &GO |
| Button2 | (Name) | btnClear |

| Control | Properties | Value |
| --- | --- | --- |
|  | Text | &Clear |
| Button3 | (Name) | btnExit |
|  | Text | E&xit |
| TextBox1 | (Name) | txtMeal |
| TextBox2 | (Name) | txtTip |

Your form should now look like the form in Figure 12.3.1.2

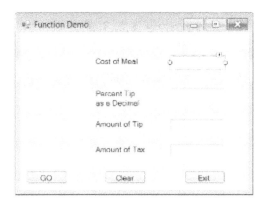

**Figure 12.3.1.2**

Now we are ready to create a function. The first function we will write will be the calcTip() function. The function is to receive two decimal numbers from the btnGO_Click Event. The first value is the cost of the meal, the second the percentage amount of the tip as a decimal value. The function will then calcualte the tip to be passed back to the calling method.

The second function will be called calcTax and will calculate the tax on the meal. The local tax is six percent. Only one value will be passed to the function, passed ByVal. This will be the cost of the meal. The function will return the amount of the tax charged on the meal amount.

To get to the code window to enter the code for the two functions go to the View menu and select Code.

Figure 12.3.1.3 shows the code for the two functions.

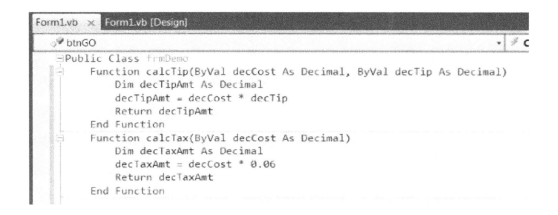

```
Form1.vb  ×  Form1.vb [Design]

btnGO

Public Class frmDemo
    Function calcTip(ByVal decCost As Decimal, ByVal decTip As Decimal)
        Dim decTipAmt As Decimal
        decTipAmt = decCost * decTip
        Return decTipAmt
    End Function
    Function calcTax(ByVal decCost As Decimal)
        Dim decTaxAmt As Decimal
        decTaxAmt = decCost * 0.06
        Return decTaxAmt
    End Function
```

***Figure 12.3.1.3***

Now code the btnGO_Click Event as shown in Figure 12.3.1.4

```
Form1.vb  X  Form1.vb [Design]

 btnGO

Public Class frmDemo
    Function calcTip(ByVal decCost As Decimal, ByVal decTip As Dec
        Dim decTipAmt As Decimal
        decTipAmt = decCost * decTip
        Return decTipAmt
    End Function
    Function calcTax(ByVal decCost As Decimal)
        Dim decTaxAmt As Decimal
        decTaxAmt = decCost * 0.06
        Return decTaxAmt
    End Function

    Private Sub btnGO_Click(ByVal sender As System.Object, ByVal e
        Dim decMeal As Decimal
        Dim dectip As Decimal
        Dim decTipAmt As Decimal
        Dim decTaxAmt As Decimal
        Dim decTotal As Decimal
        Dim strMessage As String
        decMeal = CDec(txtMeal.text)
        dectip = CDec(txtTip.Text)
        decTipAmt = calcTip(decMeal, dectip)
        decTaxAmt = calcTax(decMeal)
        lblTip.Text = decTipAmt.ToString("C")
        lblTax.Text = decTaxAmt.ToString("C")
        lblTip.Visible = True
        lblTax.Visible = True
        decTotal = decMeal + decTaxAmt + decTipAmt
        strMessage = "Total Charged: " & decTotal.ToString("C")
        MessageBox.Show(strMessage)
    End Sub
End Class
```

*Figure 12.3.1.4*

The first function call is to calcTip() will pass two decimal arguments to the function.

```
decTipAmt = calcTip(decMeal, dectip)
```

The second function call is to calcTax() passes one decimal argument to the function

```
decTaxAmt = calcTax(decMeal)
```

The calling method provides an decimal variable to store the value returned from the function.

Once the code is entered correctly, test the program. Enter the two values, cost of meal and tip percent (as a decimal) and click on the GO button. Your output should look similar to the output shown in Figure 12.3.1.5.

**Figure 12.3.1.5**

The tip and tax are calculated and then passed back to the btnGO_Click Event.  The amounts are displayed in their corresponding labels.  Then the amount of the meal, the tax and tip amounts are added and displayed in a MessageBox() function.

## 12.4 Summary

To declare a procedure, a Sub statement with an End Sub statement enclose the procedure code.  The calling procedure transfers control to the called procedure and when the called procedure has completed its task, control is returned to the instruction in the calling procedure after the statement that called it.

A function is similar to a procedure.  It is declared with a Function statement and and End Function enclosing the function code.  The calling procdure transfers control to the function and when the function completes a value is returned to the instruction from which it was called.

Arguments, also known as Parameters may be passed to either Procedures or Functions.  There are two ways to pass arguments to a procedure or function, ByVal or ByRef.

ByVal passes a copy of a value to the procedure or function and regardless of how that value is manipulated in the procedure or function, the original value remains unchanged.

ByRef gives the procedure or function access to the value in the variable in the calling method.  This allows the procedure or function to make changes directly to the contents of a variable within the calling method.

## Unit Five – Graphics

Lesson 13 - Lines and Shapes

# Lesson 13

## Lines and Shapes

### 13.1 - Overview

This lesson looks at drawing objects using code. To do this we use the Graphics object, a general purpose drawing surface along with some standard drawing tools that come with Visual Basic and Visual Studio. Some of the methods used to create graphics are pens, brushes, color, points, and fonts.

Another important issue is the concept of x, y coordinates. Controls are oriented at the location of the x and y coordinates of the top left corner. The control starts at that point and is drawn from there using other data provided to the drawing tool. The x is the distance from the left side, the y is the distance from the top.

The pen object is a drawing tool that draws lines and has a pen color and a line thickness. The brush object has a color and is used to fill in objects.

Before any graphic object can be drawn, the programmer must declare a drawing area. If the entire form is to be used:

```
Dim graphicobject As System.Drawing.Graphics = Me.CreateGraphics()
```

Later we will explore drawing within controls like a PictureBox or a TextBox.

### 13.2 - Draw Lines

The DrawLine tool is the first we will discuss. It is used to draw a line from the starting x, y coordinate to the ending x,y coordinate. A pen object is used to draw the line and is the first parameter required. The next two parameters are the starting x and y coordinates. They are followed by two more parameters for the ending coordinates of the line.

```
graphicobject.DrawLine(pen, start x, start y, stop x, stop y)
```

The following code example draws three lines on the form. The first line with a DarkOrange pen with a width of 10 pixels. The second line in DarkOliveGreen with a pen width of 10 pixels. The third line, another DarkOrange, 10 pixels wide.

## Draw Line Example Code  (GraphicsOne)

```
    Private Sub btnDraw_Click(sender As System.Object, e As System.EventArgs)
Handles btnDraw.Click

        Dim aGraphics As System.Drawing.Graphics = Me.CreateGraphics()

        Dim aPen As Pen

        Dim bPen As Pen

        aPen = New Pen(Brushes.DarkOrange, 10)

        aGraphics.DrawLine(aPen, 10, 100, 150, 100)

        bPen = New Pen(Brushes.DarkOliveGreen, 10)

        aGraphics.DrawLine(bPen, 10, 115, 150, 115)

        aPen = New Pen(Brushes.DarkOrange, 10)

        aGraphics.DrawLine(aPen, 10, 125, 150, 125)

    End Sub
```

## 13.3 - Draw a Rectangle

The DrawRectangle tool can be used to draw both rectangles and squares. It too requires a pen and is followed by the x,y coordinates for the top left corner. Lastly the width and height of the rectangle (or square).

```
graphicobject.DrawRectangle(pen, start x, start y, width, height)
```

The following code draws two rectangles. One with a DarkOrange the other with a Darkolivegreen. The first starts at x = 10 (distance in pixels from the left side of the form) and y = 100 (distance in pixels from the top of the form). The width of both rectangles is 150 pixels with a height of 100 pixels.

Draw Rectangle Example Code    (GraphicsTwo)

```
Private Sub btnDraw_Click(sender As System.Object, e As System.EventArgs)
Handles btnDraw.Click


        Dim aGraphics As System.Drawing.Graphics = Me.CreateGraphics()

        Dim aPen As Pen

        Dim bPen As Pen

        aPen = New Pen(Brushes.DarkOrange, 10)

        aGraphics.DrawRectangle(aPen, 10, 100, 150, 100)

        bPen = New Pen(Brushes.DarkOliveGreen, 10)

        aGraphics.DrawRectangle(bPen, 200, 100, 150, 100)


    End Sub
```

152

## 13.4 - Draw an Ellipse

The DrawEllipse tool parameters are exactly like the DrawRectangle tool.  Again it is used to draw both an Ellipse and a Circle.  A pen is required and the same parameters as the rectangle.  The tool constructs the ellipse within the bounds of the rectangle specified.

```
graphicobject.DrawEllipse(pen, start x, start y, width, height)
```

The following example draws two objects, the first in DarkOrange and the second in Darkolivegreen.

Draw Ellipse Example Code   (GraphicsThree)

```
    Private Sub btnDraw_Click(sender As System.Object, e As System.EventArgs)
Handles btnDraw.Click

        Dim aGraphics As System.Drawing.Graphics = Me.CreateGraphics()

        Dim aPen As Pen

        Dim bPen As Pen

        aPen = New Pen(Brushes.DarkOrange, 10)

        aGraphics.DrawEllipse(aPen, 10, 100, 150, 100)

        bPen = New Pen(Brushes.DarkOliveGreen, 10)

        aGraphics.DrawEllipse(bPen, 200, 100, 150, 100)


    End Sub
```

## 13.5 - Draw a Circle

Drawing a circle is simply defining a Square object and drawing an ellipse within those parameters.

Draw Circle Example Code    (GraphicsFour)

```
    Privae Sub btnDraw_Click(sender As System.Object, e As System.EventArgs)
Handles btnDraw.Click


        Dim aGraphics As System.Drawing.Graphics = Me.CreateGraphics()

        Dim aPen As Pen

        Dim bPen As Pen

        aPen = New Pen(Brushes.DarkOrange, 10)

        aGraphics.DrawEllipse(aPen, 10, 100, 100, 100)

        bPen = New Pen(Brushes.DarkOliveGreen, 10)

        aGraphics.DrawEllipse(bPen, 200, 100, 100, 100)


    End Sub
```

## 13.6 - Draw a Polygon

The definition of a polygon is an enclosed object with three or more sides. Triangles, Squares, Parallelograms, Pentagons, Octagons, etc. are all classified as polygons. The DrawPolygon method requires an x, y coordinate for each corner of the graphic. A triangle will have three sets of coordinates, an octagon will have eight sets of coordinates. The DrawPolygon method requires two parameters. The first is to define a pen to be used. The second is a reference to an array of Points.

```
graphicobject.DrawPolygon(pen, pointsarray)
```

Our example is drawing a polygon with five sides. An array of points is defined as aPoints. The array is initialized with five sets of x, y coordinates.

Draw Polygon Example Code (GraphicsFive)

```
    Private Sub btnDraw_Click(sender As System.Object, e As System.EventArgs)
Handles btnDraw.Click

        Dim aGraphics As System.Drawing.Graphics = Me.CreateGraphics()

        Dim aPen As Pen

        Dim A1 As New Point(10, 10)

        Dim A2 As New Point(100, 30)

        Dim A3 As New Point(150, 150)

        Dim A4 As New Point(100, 230)

        Dim A5 As New Point(15, 190)

        Dim aPoints As Point() = {A1, A2, A3, A4, A5}

        aPen = New Pen(Brushes.DarkOrange, 10)

        aGraphics.DrawPolygon(aPen, aPoints)

    End Sub
```

## 13.7 - Draw a Triangle

Drawing a triangle is accomplished with the DrawPolygon method. The array contains three sets of x, y points.

Draw Triangle Example Code (GraphicsSix)

```
Private Sub btnDraw_Click(sender As System.Object, e As System.EventArgs)
Handles btnDraw.Click


        Dim aGraphics As System.Drawing.Graphics = Me.CreateGraphics()

        Dim aPen As Pen

        Dim A1 As New Point(100, 100)

        Dim A2 As New Point(10, 300)

        Dim A3 As New Point(190, 300)

        Dim aPoints As Point() = {A1, A2, A3}

        aPen = New Pen(Brushes.DarkOrange, 10)

        aGraphics.DrawPolygon(aPen, aPoints)


    End Sub
```

## 13.8 - Draw a Pie Graphic

Another basic shape is a Pie Shaped object drawn by the DrawPie method.  To draw the object it requires a defined pen, a start X and Y location, the length of each side and two values to establish the curve of the rounded side.

Draw Pie Example Code        (GraphicsSeven)

```
    Private Sub btnDraw_Click(sender As System.Object, e As System.EventArgs)
Handles btnDraw.Click


        Dim aGraphics As System.Drawing.Graphics = Me.CreateGraphics()

        Dim aPen As Pen

        aPen = New Pen(Brushes.DarkOrange, 10)

        aGraphics.DrawPie(aPen, 30, 30, 200, 200, 0, 60)


    End Sub
```

### 13.9 - Draw in a Picturebox Conrol

Up to this point all drawings were done in the form.  Now let's explore drawing within another control.  This lesson will show how to draw in the PictureBox control.  Note the difference in the dimension where the object aGraphics is declared, it is highlighted and underlined:

To write on the form:

```
Dim aGraphics As System.Drawing.Graphics = Me.CreateGraphics()
```

To write in a PictureBox:

```
Dim aGraphics As System.Drawing.Graphics = picGraphics.CreateGraphics()
```

Yes, just change the Me. to the object name of the PictureBox.


Draw in Picture Box Example Code (GraphicsEight)

```
Private Sub btnDraw_Click(sender As System.Object, e As System.EventArgs)
Handles btnDraw.Click

    Dim aGraphics As System.Drawing.Graphics = picGraphics.CreateGraphics()

    Dim aPen As Pen

    Dim bPen As Pen

    aPen = New Pen(Brushes.DarkOrange, 7)

    aGraphics.DrawLine(aPen, 50, 100, 300, 100)

    bPen = New Pen(Brushes.DarkOliveGreen, 10)

    aGraphics.DrawLine(bPen, 50, 115, 300, 115)

    aPen = New Pen(Brushes.DarkOrange, 17)

    aGraphics.DrawLine(aPen, 50, 130, 300, 130)

End Sub
```

### 13.10 - Draw in a TextBox Control

Now let's explore drawing within another control.  This lesson will show how to draw in the TextBox control.  Note the difference in the dimension where the object aGraphics is declared, it is highlighted and underlined:

To write on the form:

```
Dim aGraphics As System.Drawing.Graphics = Me.CreateGraphics()
```

To write in a TextBox:

```
Dim aGraphics As System.Drawing.Graphics = txtLine.CreateGraphics()
```

Yes, just change the Me. to the object name of the TextBox.

Draw in TextBox Example Code     (GraphicsNine)

```
Private Sub btnDraw_Click(sender As System.Object, e As System.EventArgs) Handles btnDraw.Click

    Dim aGraphics As System.Drawing.Graphics = txtLine.CreateGraphics()

    Dim aPen As Pen

    aPen = New Pen(Brushes.red, 7)

    aGraphics.DrawLine(aPen, 5, 5, 300, 5)

End Sub
```

## 13.11 - Fill in a Graphic

All of our graphics have just been outlines. The each of the draw methods has a corresponding fill method. The fill method requires that you declare a "brush" object and specify a color. The color parameter will allow Intellesense to list all of the allowable colors.

Fill Graphics        (GraphicsTen)

```
    Private Sub btnDraw_Click(sender As System.Object, e As System.EventArgs)
Handles btnDraw.Click

        Dim aGraphics As System.Drawing.Graphics = Me.CreateGraphics()

        Dim aPen As Pen

        Dim bPen As Pen

        Dim aBrush As Brush

        aBrush = New SolidBrush(Color.LightSeaGreen)

        aPen = New Pen(Brushes.Blue, 10)

        aGraphics.DrawEllipse(aPen, 100, 100, 100, 100)

        aGraphics.FillEllipse(aBrush, 100, 100, 100, 100)

        bPen = New Pen(Brushes.Green, 10)

        aBrush = New SolidBrush(Color.BurlyWood)

        aGraphics.DrawRectangle(bPen, 300, 100, 100, 100)

        aGraphics.FillRectangle(aBrush, 300, 100, 100, 100)

    End Sub
```

## 13.12 - Draw a String

To draw text use the DrawString method. This method can take several arguments. The first argument is the reference to the string to be drawn. Next, the font used to draw the string. Then the definition of the brush to be used. Next, the x and y positions where the drawing should begin. Last, the reference to the System.Drawing.StringFormat (the format details for the string).

Sample:

```
aGraphics.DrawString(userMsg, aFont, aBrush, 100, 100, aFormat)
```

The font object may look like this:

```
Dim aFont As Font

aFont = New System.Drawing.Font("Verdana", 20, FontStyle.Italic)
```

The brush object:

```
Dim aBrush As Brush

aBrush = New Drawing.SolidBrush(Color.Chocolate)
```

And the Format object:

```
Dim aFormat As New System.Drawing.StringFormat
```

The text to be drawn could be either a string literal or the contents of a string variable.

## Draw String Example Code  (Graphics)

```
Private Sub Button1_Click(sender As System.Object, e As System.EventArgs) Handles
Button1.Click

        Dim aGraphics As System.Drawing.Graphics = Me.CreateGraphics()

        Dim aFont As Font

        Dim aBrush As Brush

        Dim userMsg As String

        Dim aFormat As New System.Drawing.StringFormat

        userMsg = InputBox("What do you want to say?", "Data Entry Form",

                        "Enter message here", 100, 100)
```

```
    aBrush = New Drawing.SolidBrush(Color.Chocolate)

    aFont = New System.Drawing.Font("Verdana", 20, FontStyle.Italic)

    aGraphics.DrawString(userMsg, aFont, aBrush, 100, 100, aFormat)

    aBrush.Dispose()

    aFont.Dispose()

    aGraphics.Dispose()

End Sub
```

### 13.13 - Draw with the Mouse

Using the mouse click to draw an object is as simple as putting what you have learned so far about drawing objects in a new event. The "MouseDown" event is accessed from the code window. Select (Form1.Events) from the Class Name drop-down box, then select MouseDown from the Method Name drop-down list.

Now enter the code shown below to draw a rectangle with a coral border and filled with the color DarkOrange.

Draw with the Mouse Example Code  (GraphicsTwelve)

```
    Private Sub Form1_MouseDown(sender As Object, e As
System.Windows.Forms.MouseEventArgs) Handles Me.MouseDown

        Dim aGraphics As System.Drawing.Graphics = Me.CreateGraphics()

        Dim aPen As Pen

        Dim aBrush As Brush

        aBrush = New SolidBrush(Color.Coral)

        aPen = New Pen(Brushes.DarkOrange, 10)

        aGraphics.DrawRectangle(aPen, e.X, e.Y, 150, 100)

        aGraphics.FillRectangle(aBrush, e.X, e.Y, 150, 100)

    End Sub
```

## 13.14 – Determining the Mouse Location

The MouseDown event returns a number of useful values. The most useful is the event returns the x and y coordinates locating the grid location where the button was clicked. This can be used in your code to draw objects on the form wherever the buttons are clicked.

Once a position is found it can be used as the starting position for various objects. Objects are defined by the location relative to a starting point. This means you can use this information to create objects that are made up of any combination of shapes and lines.

The example in section 16.13 uses the location information. The event object is returned as a variable named e. This variable has an X and Y property which are the coordinates that hold the location where the mouse was clicked. Note the declaration of the e variable in the header of the MouseDown event:

```
Private Sub Form1_MouseDown(sender As Object, e As
System.Windows.Forms.MouseEventArgs) Handles Me.MouseDown
```

The X and Y properties of the e variable are used in the code lines:

```
aGraphics.DrawRectangle(aPen, e.X, e.Y, 150, 100)

aGraphics.FillRectangle(aBrush, e.X, e.Y, 150, 100)
```

The e.X and e.Y can be used to establish drawing points for any type of shape or line. These X and Y properties are also established on the MouseUp event.

The MouseButton.Left and MouseButton.Right may be used to determine which mouse button was pressed. This allows the program to take different actions for the left mouse button and the right mouse button.

## 13.15 – Styling the Pen Object

The pen object can draw different line styles.  There are 5 defined styles plus a custom style for other combinations of line styles.  The styles are:

Dot

Dash

DashDot

DashDotDot

Solid

Custom

## Styling the Pen Example Code  (GraphicsThirteen)

```
Private Sub btnDraw_Click(sender As System.Object, e As System.EventArgs)
Handles btnDraw.Click

    Dim aGraphics As System.Drawing.Graphics = Me.CreateGraphics()

    Dim aPen As Pen

    Dim bPen As Pen

    aPen = New Pen(Brushes.DarkOrange, 10)

    aPen.DashStyle = Drawing.Drawing2D.DashStyle.Dot

    aGraphics.DrawRectangle(aPen, 10, 100, 150, 100)

    bPen = New Pen(Brushes.DarkOliveGreen, 10)

    bPen.DashStyle = Drawing.Drawing2D.DashStyle.Dash

    aGraphics.DrawRectangle(bPen, 200, 100, 150, 100)

End Sub
```

### 13.16 – Clearing the Form

There are two ways to clear a form. The first is the clear method. This method takes as a parameter the color that will be used to replace objects on the form. The BackColor property of the form is most commonly used for this purpose. Another way to clear a form is to draw new shapes over existing shapes using the BackGround Color of the form.

Using the BackColor property of the form, the clear method will work, even if the program has changed the BackColor property while running.

Clearing the Form Example Code  (GraphicsFourteen)

```
    Private Sub btnClear_Click(sender As System.Object, e As System.EventArgs)
Handles btnClear.Click

        ' Create a new graphic object

        Dim g As Graphics = Me.CreateGraphics

        g.Clear(Me.BackColor)

    End Sub
```

### 13.17 – Summary

In this lesson on graphics, we have learned to create some basic shapes.  The rectangle shape is also used to create a square or a rectangle.  The ellipse shape is used to create both an ellipse and a circle.  The polygon shape is used to create any three or more sided object.  Establish each point in an array and draw the object.  Not only are graphics used to draw shapes, but also strings.

We looked at pens and brushes and when each is used.  Giving the pen a width and color to draw a line.  Giving the brush a color to fill a object.

Another topic was learning to use the MouseDown and MouseUp events to return the X and Y coordinates of the mouse location.  The e variable has the X and Y coordinates as properties and can be saved from the e.X and e.Y values.  Since all graphics objects are located by their top left coordinate or the points of each corner in an array or a start and end point of a line, we can use this information to draw objects on the screen based on the information returned by the MouseUp and MouseDown events.

# PRACTICE PROBLEMS

This section contains practice problems for each lesson.  While there were Step-By-Step Exercises embedded in each lesson, more practice is needed to insure the ability to use the concepts learned.  This is where practice problems comes in.

As you finish each lesson, find the matching set of practice problems in this section and make sure you can solve those problems with a Visual Basic.NET project.

# Lesson 1

## 3 Exercises (IDE, picBox1, picBox2)

*IDE*
Using the Visual Basic.NET IDE

Open Microsoft Visual Studio 2013
    Select "New Project"
        Under "Installed Templates" Select Visual Basic.
    Select "Windows Forms Applications.
    Change Name: to MyTest
    Click on: OK
    Click on the middle of "Form1"

        Change Text Property to: My New Form
        Change (name) Property to: MyForm

In the Toolbox under Common Controls, double click on: Label and move the resulting control to the center of the form.

        Change (Name) Property to: lblName
        Change Text Property to:  --Enter your name--

In the Toolbox under Common Controls, double click on: Button and move the resulting control to the center of the form between the label and the bottom of the form.

        Change (Name) Property to: btnExit
        Change Text Property to:  Exit

    Double Click on the Exit button to get to the code window.
        Between
            Private Sub btnExit_Click(sender.....)
            and
            End Sub
    Add the code line:  Me.Close()
    Click on the menu item Debug (at the top of Visual Studio)
    Select "Start Debugging" from the drop down menu.
    Your form should run...

### *Guidelines for Saving VB Lab Exercises*

When you complete an VB Programming Exercise you will have created a new file and a new folder.  By default these are created in a User Project Folder.  The file should be named as indicated in the lab.  To copy your work to another folder, removable device or to the cloud (Dropbox, SkyDrive, etc.), follow these directions:

Know where you saved your project
Find and Select the folder, you need to move the ENTIRE folder to move your work.
    Right Click on the Folder.
    From the Pop Up Menu select the "Copy" menu choice.
    Open the folder in which you want to save the folder being copied.
    Right click in that folder and select "Paste" from the popup menu.
    You MUST have the ENTIRE folder as the Project is made up of many files.
    Double clicking on the .sln file in the folder will start Visual Basic and load the project.


### *Finding and using the Executable (.exe) File*

When you successfully compile your Visual Basic program you will create an executable(.exe) file that can be moved and executed to any other computer that has the .NET framework installed.  To do this follow the following steps.

    You have just completed a project named "MyTest"

    Find the folder named "MyTest" and open it.
    There will be a subfolder named "MyTest", open this folder.
    There will be a subfolder named "bin", open this folder.
    There will be a subfolder named "Debug", open this folder.
    In this folder you will find a file named "MyTest" Type of "Application",  THIS IS IT!

For the next two projects in this exercise.  I recommend you practice these exercises until you can do them without any problems. Understanding these processes are key to doing further lab exercises.

## PROJECT I
Start an Existing VB Program from the .sln file.
Unzip the picBox.zip
Open the picBox folder
Find the .sln file and double-click.
You may have to double click on the Form1 in the Solution Explorer (pane in upper right of IDE).


## PROJECT II
Start an Existing VB Program from the Start Menu
Now that you have already opened the picBox application, it should show up
under the Recent Projects. It may also be in the Open Projects selection.

Find the application on the Start Page and start the application.

# Lesson 2
# 4 Projects (IDE, Snap Lines, New Form, Acme)

## Project 1:  The Visual Basic IDE

Identify the numbered parts of the IDE

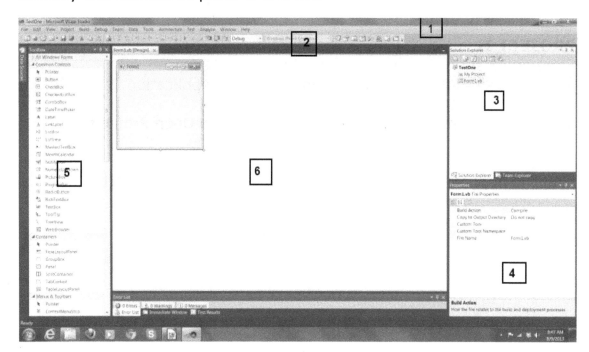

1. _____

2. _____

3. _____

4. _____

5. _____

6. _____

## Project 2:  Snap Lines

As the control moves, **_snap lines_**, these lines do what?

Blue lines show:

Red lines show:

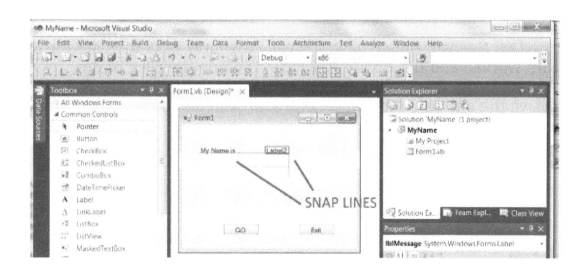

**Project 3:  Create a New Form**

Name the form **frmAverage** and set the text property to **Average Sales**

Set up a form that will accept 4 inputs into TextBoxes
Name them **txtSales1, txtSales2, txtSales3, and txtSales4**

Place a label next to each textbox.  Label the textboxes as follows:
>    **Sales Quarter 1**
>    **Sales Quarter 2**
>    **Sales Quarter 3**
>    **Sales Quarter 4**

Put a label on the form to contain the Average Sales.  Label should have a Fixed 3D border.  Name the label **lblAverage**,  A blank text property and AutoSize should be false.

Place 3 buttons on the form.
| | |
|---|---|
| **btnCalc** | Text: **Calculate** |
| **btnClear** | Text: **Clear** |
| **btnExit** | Text: **Exit** |

**Project 4: Acme Payroll Program.**

Acme Ltd. Needs a simple payroll form.  It simply asks the user for the Hours Worked and the Hourly Pay Rate, then on the click of the Calculate Gross Pay button, multiplies the Hours by the Rate and displays the answer in the label control provided.  To close the form the user clicks on the Close button.

Set up the form as follows:

| Control | (Name) | Text | Visible |
|---|---|---|---|
| Form | frmPay | Payroll | True |
| Label | lblTitle | Acme Ltd. Payroll | True |
| Label | lblHours | Hours Worked | True |

174

| Control | (Name) | Text | Visible |
|---------|--------|------|---------|
| Label | lblRate | Hourly Pay Rate | True |
| Label | lblAns | Blank | False |
| TextBox | txtHours | Blank | True |
| TextBox | txtRate | Blank | True |
| Button | cmdCalc | Calculate Gross Pay | True |
| Button | cmdClose | Close | True |

The form should look like this:

Code for the Close button Click Event:

```
Me.Close()
```

Code for the Calculate Gross Pay button Click Event:

```
Dim decAmt As Decimal
Dim decRate As Decimal
Dim decGross As Decimal
decAmt = CDec(txtHours.Text)
decRate = CDec(txtRate.Text)
decGross = decAmt * decRate
lblAns.Text = decGross
lblAns.Visible = True
```

Enter 40 in Hours worked, 10.00 in Hourly Pay Rate. Then, click on the buttin named "Calculate Gross Pay".

# Lesson 3
## 3 Exercises (Stooges, Parks, Blue Wagon)

### PROJECT I
### *The Three Stooges*

Create a form with the following controls

| Control | (Name) | Text |
|---|---|---|
| Form | frmTTS | Stooges |
| Label | lblTitle | The Three Stooges |
| Label | lblMessage | Blank |
| Button | cmdExit | Exit |

| Control | (Name) | Image |
|---|---|---|
| PictureBox | picMoe | moe.jpg |
| PictureBox | picLarry | larry.jpg |
| PictureBox | picCurley | curley.jpg |

Create a click event for each PictureBox and display as follows:

Click on moe.jpg and display "Moe Howard" in lblMessage.text
Click on larry.jpg and display "Larry Fein" in lblMessage.text
Click on curley.jpg and display "Curley Howard" in lblMessage.text

The EXIT button should close the form.

### PROJECT II
Create a form with the following controls:

| Control | (Name) | Text |
|---|---|---|
| Form | frmPix | Parks |
| Label | lblTitle | National Parks |
| Label | lblDirections | blank |
| Button | cmdExit | Exit |
| Button | cmdBack | Change Color |
| Button | cmdPark1 | Park 1 |
| Button | cmdPark2 | Park 2 |
| Button | cmdPark3 | Park 3 |

| Control | (Name) | Image |
| --- | --- | --- |
| PictureBox | picPark1 | |
| PictureBox | picPark2 | |
| PictureBox | picPark3 | |

Do some research on National Parks and select three that interest you. Get pictures of each park and gather some information (Park Name, State where it is located) on each to include in your program.

When the user clicks on each Park button the picture of the park appears on the form and a MessageBox appears giving the name of the park and the state in which it is located.

Click on the Change Color Button and the background changes to the color of your choice.

The EXIT button must close the form.

## PROJECT III
### *The Blue Wagon*

Create a form with the following:

1. A form with the Text Property = Show and Hide, a Name property of frmShow.

2. On the form the following controls:

   a. A title label with the title of the form: The Blue Wagon

   b. A picture box containing the picture: Wagon.jpg

   c. Three buttons

      c.i. Show – Red with white text

      c.ii. Hide – Blue with Yellow text

      c.iii. Exit – White with Green text

3. When the show button is pressed change the visible property of the picture to true.

4. When the hide button is pressed change the visible property of the picture to false.

5. When the exit button is pressed, the form is closed.

6. The form borderstyle should be FixedSingle.

7. Lock all of the controls when finished.

When Finished the form should look like this:

# Lesson 4

## 3 Exercises (Calculator, CarPool, Circumference)

### Simple Rainfall Calculator

Create the form for a rainfall calculator that asks for five numbers for the total rainfall for each of five weeks.

In the code area create variables for:

> 5 variables to store rainfall (there may be fractional data)

> 1 variable to hold the sum of the 5 rainfall variables.

> 1 variable to hold the average rainfall

The form should have a Calculate, Clear and Exit Button

The form should have buttons to:

> Calculate      Calculates the average rainfall. (Green Button)

> Clear      Clears the input, date, and answer controls and puts the cursor back in the first text box. (Yellow Button)

> Exit      Exits the program (Red Button)

Buttons should be keyboard activated:

> Alt + C = Calculate

> Alt + r = Clear

> Alt + x = Exit

Accept Button should be the Calculate Button

Cancel Button should be the Exit Button

Save form for the next lesson's exercises

## Car Pool Calculator

The office is considering running a car pool.  Each car is to have 3 to 4 passengers.  Have the user enter the following information:

Number of Passengers

Miles Driven each day

Average miles per gallon

Cost per gallon of gas (enter as dollars and cents ex: 3.59)

Parking & Tolls (if any in dollars and cents ex: 1.50)

Create the form for data entry and name the controls appropriately

The answer should be displayed in a label.

There should be three buttons:

Calculate    Calculates the cost per passenger.   (Blue Button background, white letters)

Clear         Clears the input and answer controls and puts the cursor back in the first input text box.  (Green Button background, yellow letters)

Exit          Exits the program  (Red Button background, white letters.

Buttons should be keyboard activated:

Alt + C = Calculate

Alt + r = Clear

Alt + x = Exit

Accept Button should be Calculate

Cancel Button should be Exit

The code area should have the following variables

variable for number of passengers

variable for miles driven each day

variable for average miles per gallon

variable for cost per gallon of gas

variable for parking and tolls cost

variable for Cost Per Passenger

Save form for the next lesson's exercises.


## Circumference Problem


Generate a form that will take the information from the user to calculate the circumference of a round flower garden and then show the cost of three different types of fences.  One costs 12.10 per foot, the second costs 15.15 per foot and the third costs 22.89 per foot.

The user will enter the diameter of the circular garden.

The circumference, the cost per foot and the total cost should be isplayed in a label, one label for each.

There should be three buttons:

Calculate        Calculates the cost for each of the types of fence.   (Blue Button background, white letters)

Clear              Clears the input and answer controls and puts the cursor back in the first input text box.  (Green Button background, yellow letters)

Exit               Exits the program  (Red Button background, white letters.

Buttons should be keyboard activated:

Alt + C = Calculate

Alt + r = Clear

Alt + x = Exit

Accept Button should be Calculate

Cancel Button should be Exit

The code area should have the following variables assigned.

Variable for Cost Fence #1  $12.10

Variable for Cost Fence #2  $15.15

Variable for Cost Fence #3  $22.89

Variable to store the Diameter

Variable to store the Circumference

Variable to store the Cost for Fence #1

Variable to store the Cost for Fence $2

Variable to store the Cost for Fence #3

Constant to store the value of PI for circumference calculation (3.14)

Save form for the next lesson's exercises.

# Lesson 5

## 3 Exercises (Calculator, CarPool, Circumference)

## Simple Rainfall Calculator

Complete the program you began in Week 4. Write the code to take the 5 rainfall values from the form, calculate the average and display the average on the form.

Use the following values for your test:

> Rainfall values:  .07; 0.1; 1.0; 0; 2.1

## Car Pool Calculator

Complete the exercise  you began in Week 4

The office is considering running a car pool.  Each car is to have 3 to 4 passengers.  Have the user enter the following information:

> Number of Passengers
>
> Miles Driven each day
>
> Average miles per gallon
>
> Cost per gallon of gas (enter as dollars and cents ex: 3.59)
>
> Parking & Tolls (if any in dollars and cents ex: 1.50)

Calculate the cost per person to do this car pool

Miles Driven divided by the average miles per gallon.

Multiply the result by the cost per gallon of gas.

Add Parking and tolls to the result

Divide the result by the number of passengers

Display the answer in a label.

Use the following values for your test:

| | |
|---|---|
| Number of Passengers | 3 |
| Miles Driven each day | 17 |
| Average miles per gallon | 24 |
| Cost per gallon of gas | 2.39 |
| Parking and Tolls | 10.50 |

## Circumference

Complete the Lab you began in Week 4. Calculate the Circumference of the circular garden and then calculate the cost of each grade of fencing.

Display the circumference, the price of the fence and the cost to circle the entire garden with that grade of fence. There should be one display for each grade of fence.

Use the following values for your test:

| | |
|---|---|
| Circumference | 13 |

# Lesson 6

# 4 Exercises (Concatenation, Converter, Planet, Years)

## Name Concatenation

Part I:  Create a form thal has two text boxes where the user enters a first name and a last name.  When the GO button is clicked, the first and last names are displayed in a label on the form.  There should be a clear and exit button as well.

Part II:     Same as Part I except the name is displayed in a MessageBox with a Caption = Name Concatenation.  Just the OK button on the MessageBox.

When testing Part I and Part II, enter your first and last names.

## Money Converter

Create a form that allows the user to enter a dollar amount.  Then convert the dollar amount into the following currencies and display the calculated amount.  Show all amounts to two decimal places.  There should be a clear and exit button as well.

Canada = 1.086

UK = 0.595

Russia = 34.745

Mexico = 12.893

Japan = 101.545

Euro = 0.730

Show all the converted amounts on the same form.

Test with the dollar amount $3.00

## Planet Weight

Create a form that allows the user to enter their weight. Then calculate the persons weight on the following multipliers for the listed planets and display the calculated weight IN A MESSAGEBOX.

| Mercury | 0.37 |
|---------|------|
| Venus | 0.88 |
| Mars | 0.38 |
| Jupiter | 2.64 |
| Saturn | 1.20 |
| Uranus | 1.15 |
| Neptune | 1.12 |

When the MessageBox shows the calculated weight it should display the information icon, Caption = Your Weight, and the OK and Cancel Buttons. You do not need to do anything with the Cancel button. The message should read

'Your Weight on XXXXXX is 999999'

Test using the weight of 200 pounds.


## Dog Years

Create a form that allows the user to enter their age in years. The program should multiply the years times seven (7) and display the age in dog years. There should be a clear and exit button as well.

Test with the age: 22

# Lesson 7

## Decisions

## 4 Exercises (Spring Break, Photocopy, Planet, Years)

### Spring Break

The college is offering three different trips for spring break. Trip One to Key West Florida costs $1,100 per person. Trip Two to Cancun Mexico costs $1,440.00 per person. Trip Three to St. Maarten costs $1,990.00 per person. Create a form that allows users to select one of the trips from a checkbox, calculate the tax at 6% and display the tax and the total cost in label controls. There should be a Calculate Button to do the calculation and a Exit button to quit the program.

Test all three choices

### Photocopy

Develop a program to calculate the costs for copying documents in your copy center. Enter the number of copies made in a textbox. Then based on the table below, calculate the cost for that number of copies. Display the copy cost, the tax (6%), and the total (cost + tax) in three different label controls. Each of those labels should indicate what is being displayed in that label.

| Number of Copies | Price per Copy |
|---|---|
| 1 – 100 | 0.15 |
| 101 – 500 | 0.11 |
| 501 – 1,000 | 0.07 |
| > 1,000 | 0.06 |

Test using Number of copies: 25 and 750

## Planet Weight

Create a form that allows the user to enter their weight and then select a planet using RadioButtons.  Then calculate the persons weight on the following multipliers for the listed planets and display the calculated weight IN A LABEL CONTROL.  The switch statement should be used to determine the weight entered on the Planet selected

| | |
|---|---|
| Mercury | 0.37 |
| Venus | 0.88 |
| Mars | 0.38 |
| Jupiter | 2.64 |
| Saturn | 1.20 |
| Uranus | 1.15 |
| Neptune | 1.12 |

Test runs on the following planets:

Mercury

Jupiter

Uranus

## Animal Years

Change the Dog years application to include two more animals, Cows and Mice.  The form should accept the human's age in years, and the months since the last birthday.  Then a button to calculate the age in months and display in a label.

Once this step has been completed, a group box should appear with the title 'Select an Animal' with three choices; Dog, Cow, and Mouse. There should be two buttons Calculate and Exit.  THIS PART OF THE FORM SHOULD NOT BE VISIBLE UNTIL THE AGE IN MONTHS HAS BEEN CALCULATED.  The user can select one of the animals and click on the Calculate button and the human's age should be converted to that animals age factor and displayed in a label.

Dog years factor is 7 years to 1 human year.

Cow years factor is 5 years to 1 human year.

Mouse years factor is 25 years to 1 human year.

Animal years = (factor * human months) / 12

Test using the age factor of 18 years for each animal (Dog, Cow, Mouse)

# Lesson 8

## Repetition

## 3 Exercises (Pennies, Sum, Distance)

### Pennies for Pay

You have been hired to work on a job that pays every day. The agreement is that the employer will pay you as follows: .01 for your first day, .02 for your second day, .04 for your third day, .08 for your fourth day and so on, doubling your pay each day you work. The form should display in a ListBox Control the pay for each of 30 days, formatted as Currency. When the user clicks on the Calculate button the pay for the given number of days should be calculated and displayed in a MessageBox as follows:

Example:

| | | |
|---|---|---|
| Enter 1 Day, Show: | Day 1: | $.01 |
| Enter 2 Days, Show: | Day 2: | $.02 |
| Enter 4 Days, Show: | Day 4: | $.08 |

Test using the following number of days:   10,  15, 30

### Sum of Numbers

Create an application that has a Calculate Button and an Exit Button.

When the Calculate Button is clicked an InputBox opens and asks the user 'Enter a positive integer:' the number is added to a variable and then the next number is requested. This process is repeated until ten (10) numbers have been input.  Use a DO WHILE loop structure to create this loop.

After all the numbers have been entered, display the sum of the numbers in a MessageBox as shown below:

### *'The SUM of the 10 numbers entered is: 999'*

Where 999 is the sum you calculated.

Test with the following numbers:  5, 26, 341, 99, 0, 222, 86, 111, 9, 101

## Distance Calculator

This program will calculate the distance a vehicle will travel in a given distance.  The formula is:     *Distance = Speed * Time*.

The user will enter the Speed and Time (in hours) in textboxes.  The Distance traveled each hour of the trip will then be calculated and displayed in a ListBox control.

Example Output:

60 mph for 3 hours

Hour 1:     60 miles

Hour 2:     120 miles

Hour 3:     180 miles

Test with the following:

| SPEED | TIME |
|---|---|
| 60 | 2 hours |
| 70 | 2 hours |
| 55 | 3 hours |

# Lesson 9

## Arrays

## 4 Exercises (Stats, Grades, Phone, Numbers)

### Sales Statistics

The Acme Corp. Keeps track of sales monthly for each year. Create a form and an application that will accept 4 monthly sales for 2012 and store them in an array. The user will enter each months sales in an inputbox. Make sure each inputbox message includes the month for which the sales will be entered. Example 'Enter sales for Month 1'.

After all sales have been entered, display the following:

Total Sales

Average Monthly Sales

Month and Amount of Highest Sales

Month and Amount of Lowest Sales

All dollar amounts must be formatted as currency.

Test with the following sales data:

122,399.59

357,925.44

299,987.30

101,528.72

# Grade Book

Create an application to allow Prof. Smith to enter the grades for each student in his Networking class. Use parallel arrays for the Student name, Mid Term Grade and Final Grade. There are 6 students in his class. Enter the following data in the arrays.

| Student Name | Mid-Term | Final |
|---|---|---|
| Mike Rowe | 88 | 92 |
| Donna Drive | 94 | 99 |
| Ed Volt | 77 | 77 |
| Sam Sharpe | 88 | 92 |
| Sue Pascal | 84 | 95 |
| Jon Dough | 56 | 87 |

After all information has been entered, display the following on a from.

Mid-Term and Final Grade for each student

Letter Grade for each student:

A = 90 to 100

B = 80 to 89

C = 70 to 79

D = 60 to 69

F < 60

Indicate Student with highest mid-term grade

Indicate Student with higest final grade

## Phone Book

The program should have two arrays (parallel arrays).  The first array should have 5 phone numbers (seven digits without the dash), the second should have the 5 names (first and last names) associated with each phone number.

When the user types a phone number into the textbox on the form the name of the person should pop up in a MessageBox.

## Number Analysis

The user enters 6 numbers using InputBox functions.  The numbers are stored in an array.  When all the numbers have been entered the program should display the following in a listbox control on the form.

Total of all numbers entered

The Average of all numbers entered

The highest number entered

The lowest number entered

The form must have properly labeled answers in the List box.

Example:   The Highest Number Entered:  12345

The form should have a Start Button, a Clear Button and an Exit Button.

Test Data:

| 597 | 489 | 922 | 54 | 0 | 1492 |
|-----|-----|-----|-----|-----|-----|

# Lesson 10

## Menus

## 4 Exercises (Menu, Color, Application, Pictures )

### Generate Menu System

Create a form with the following menu system.  Name the menu items using proper prefix (mnu) and should include the following elements:

| File | Edit | Help | |
|------|------|------|---|
| New | Undo | About | |
| Open | ReDo | Help | |
| Close | Cut | | Online |
| Save | Copy | | System |
| Save As | Paste | | Links |
| Print | | Support | |
| Exit | | | |

Check marks in the Help menu (all sub menu items under Help)

Separator bars

> After Close
>
> After Save As
>
> After Print
>
> After ReDo

No code required for any of the menu items.

## Color Selection

Create a menu system that has three main categories. (File, Color, About). The File dropdown should have only the 'Exit' Command. The Color dropdown should show a list of six different colors. Clicking on a color should change the background of the form to that color and also place a check next to the color selected in the menu. The About menu item should place your name in an invisible label on the form and then make the label visible.

## Choose an Application

Create an form that has a menu system with three main categories. (File, Operation, Help).

The File dropdown should only have the 'Exit' Command.

The Operation Dropdown should have 4 choices. (Add, Subtract, Multiply, and Divide).

The Form should have text boxes for two numbers and a label to display the answer.

When the user has placed numbers in each of the textboxes, they will go to the Menu item Operation and select the math option they wish to perform on the two numbers. When the operation is complete, the result will be placed in the label on the form and then the label will be made visible.

The Help option will have one sub menu item 'Clear'. When this is selected, the two textboxes and the label on the form will be cleared and the label will be made invisible.

## Pictures

Create a form with six (6) picture boxes (find pictures on the internet, in good taste). Pictures should not be visible when the form starts. Create a menu system to show each picture in its picture box, make sure it makes any other visible picture, invisble. No two pictures should be visible at the same time (only one picture visible at a time). Each picture should have a RANDOM background color.

# Lesson 11

# Multiple Forms

# 4 Exercises (Multi-Form, Splash, Modal, Modeless)

## Multi-Form Application

Using a copy of the project you created in Lesson 11.1 Step-By-Step. As a base application for this project. Add a top level menu item called Test with two sublevel menus, Modal and Modeless.

Submit:

Screenshot of form showing the menu item Test with its two sublevel menus.

## Splash Form

Add a Splash Screen to your application that contains the following text:

CMP 117 Visual Basic

Multiple Forms Lab

Your name here

The form background should be a bright color and the text should have sufficent contrast to be very readable.

## Modal Form

When the Modal menu item is clicked, open a Modal Form containing the following information:

A Simulated Error

Your name here

Use the About Form and change the text on the form using code.

## Modeless Form

When the Modless menu item is clicked, open a Modeless Form containing the following text:

Your Subscription is about to Expire.

Please Reply Promptly

Thank You

Your name here

Use the About Form and change the text on the form using code.

# Lesson 12

## Procedures and Functions

## Exercises (Name, Interest, Course Cost )

### Name Procedure

Create a procedure that receives 3 arguments (First Name, Middle Name, and Last Name. The procedure should concatenate the three arguments and produce a messagebox containing the concatenated name.

Write a VB program that accepts the arguments into textboxes on a form, and then passes the first, middle and last names to the procedure.

### Interest Function

Write functions that when given the principal amount, rate of interest and term of the loan, calculates the:

>  Simple interest on a the loan.

>  Total paid on the loan (principal and interest)

>  A monthly payment

Create a form that will allow for the entry of the principal, rate and term. Then code to call the functions to display the results on the form in label controls.

### Course Cost

Write a program with a form that asks the user for the following information.

>  Student ID:
>  Student Last Name:
>  Student First Name:

Name of the Course:
     (Example:  Intro. To Programming)
Course ID:
     (Example:  CMP104)
Number of Credits
     (Example: 3)

Create a function that calculates the cost of the course and returns that value to the main program.  Use the amount $238.00 as the cost per credit.

Create a procedure that displays a messagebox with the following information:

Concatenated first and last name of the student
Student ID
Course ID and Course Name
Number of credits, Cost per credit,
Total cost for the course.

EXAMPLE

     Jon Dough
     12345
     CMP104 – Intro to Programming
     3 credits at $238.00 per credit
     Total Course Cost:  $714.00

# Lesson 13

## Graphics

## 2 Exercises (Picture, Mouse)

### Create A Picture

Using as many different graphics as you can, from the lessons on graphics, create a scene.  Be Creative!

Set up a form 600 X 600

Place your picture on the form.  Use different shapes, use color, use your imagination.

There should be three buttons at the bottom of the form.  First button executes the code to draw the picture.  The second button clears the form and the last button exits the form.

### Draw a Picture using the Mouse

In Lesson 13 we learned how to use the mouse to click on the form and place a graphic object on the form.

Set up a form 600 x 600

Using the menu system (Lesson 11), create menu selections for five (5) different graphics.

When the user selects a graphic from the menu and clicks on the form, that graphics object appears on the form.

There should also be menu items that will clear the form and exit the form.

# APPENDIX

## *APPENDIX A - ASCII CHART*

| Char | Dec | Oct | Hex | | Char | Dec | Oct | Hex | | Char | Dec | Oct | Hex | | Char | Dec | Oct | Hex |
|------|-----|-----|-----|---|------|-----|-----|-----|---|------|-----|-----|-----|---|------|-----|-----|-----|
| (nul) | 0 | 0000 | 0x00 | | (sp) | 32 | 0040 | 0x20 | | @ | 64 | 0100 | 0x40 | | ` | 96 | 0140 | 0x60 |
| (soh) | 1 | 0001 | 0x01 | | ! | 33 | 0041 | 0x21 | | A | 65 | 0101 | 0x41 | | a | 97 | 0141 | 0x61 |
| (stx) | 2 | 0002 | 0x02 | | " | 34 | 0042 | 0x22 | | B | 66 | 0102 | 0x42 | | b | 98 | 0142 | 0x62 |
| (etx) | 3 | 0003 | 0x03 | | # | 35 | 0043 | 0x23 | | C | 67 | 0103 | 0x43 | | c | 99 | 0143 | 0x63 |
| (eot) | 4 | 0004 | 0x04 | | $ | 36 | 0044 | 0x24 | | D | 68 | 0104 | 0x44 | | d | 100 | 0144 | 0x64 |
| (enq) | 5 | 0005 | 0x05 | | % | 37 | 0045 | 0x25 | | E | 69 | 0105 | 0x45 | | e | 101 | 0145 | 0x65 |
| (ack) | 6 | 0006 | 0x06 | | & | 38 | 0046 | 0x26 | | F | 70 | 0106 | 0x46 | | f | 102 | 0146 | 0x66 |
| (bel) | 7 | 0007 | 0x07 | | ' | 39 | 0047 | 0x27 | | G | 71 | 0107 | 0x47 | | g | 103 | 0147 | 0x67 |
| (bs) | 8 | 0010 | 0x08 | | ( | 40 | 0050 | 0x28 | | H | 72 | 0110 | 0x48 | | h | 104 | 0150 | 0x68 |
| (ht) | 9 | 0011 | 0x09 | | ) | 41 | 0051 | 0x29 | | I | 73 | 0111 | 0x49 | | i | 105 | 0151 | 0x69 |
| (nl) | 10 | 0012 | 0x0a | | * | 42 | 0052 | 0x2a | | J | 74 | 0112 | 0x4a | | j | 106 | 0152 | 0x6a |
| (vt) | 11 | 0013 | 0x0b | | + | 43 | 0053 | 0x2b | | K | 75 | 0113 | 0x4b | | k | 107 | 0153 | 0x6b |
| (np) | 12 | 0014 | 0x0c | | , | 44 | 0054 | 0x2c | | L | 76 | 0114 | 0x4c | | l | 108 | 0154 | 0x6c |
| (cr) | 13 | 0015 | 0x0d | | - | 45 | 0055 | 0x2d | | M | 77 | 0115 | 0x4d | | m | 109 | 0155 | 0x6d |
| (so) | 14 | 0016 | 0x0e | | . | 46 | 0056 | 0x2e | | N | 78 | 0116 | 0x4e | | n | 110 | 0156 | 0x6e |
| (si) | 15 | 0017 | 0x0f | | / | 47 | 0057 | 0x2f | | O | 79 | 0117 | 0x4f | | o | 111 | 0157 | 0x6f |
| (dle) | 16 | 0020 | 0x10 | | 0 | 48 | 0060 | 0x30 | | P | 80 | 0120 | 0x50 | | p | 112 | 0160 | 0x70 |
| (dc1) | 17 | 0021 | 0x11 | | 1 | 49 | 0061 | 0x31 | | Q | 81 | 0121 | 0x51 | | q | 113 | 0161 | 0x71 |
| (dc2) | 18 | 0022 | 0x12 | | 2 | 50 | 0062 | 0x32 | | R | 82 | 0122 | 0x52 | | r | 114 | 0162 | 0x72 |
| (dc3) | 19 | 0023 | 0x13 | | 3 | 51 | 0063 | 0x33 | | S | 83 | 0123 | 0x53 | | s | 115 | 0163 | 0x73 |
| (dc4) | 20 | 0024 | 0x14 | | 4 | 52 | 0064 | 0x34 | | T | 84 | 0124 | 0x54 | | t | 116 | 0164 | 0x74 |
| (nak) | 21 | 0025 | 0x15 | | 5 | 53 | 0065 | 0x35 | | U | 85 | 0125 | 0x55 | | u | 117 | 0165 | 0x75 |
| (syn) | 22 | 0026 | 0x16 | | 6 | 54 | 0066 | 0x36 | | V | 86 | 0126 | 0x56 | | v | 118 | 0166 | 0x76 |
| (etb) | 23 | 0027 | 0x17 | | 7 | 55 | 0067 | 0x37 | | W | 87 | 0127 | 0x57 | | w | 119 | 0167 | 0x77 |
| (can) | 24 | 0030 | 0x18 | | 8 | 56 | 0070 | 0x38 | | X | 88 | 0130 | 0x58 | | x | 120 | 0170 | 0x78 |
| (em) | 25 | 0031 | 0x19 | | 9 | 57 | 0071 | 0x39 | | Y | 89 | 0131 | 0x59 | | y | 121 | 0171 | 0x79 |
| (sub) | 26 | 0032 | 0x1a | | : | 58 | 0072 | 0x3a | | Z | 90 | 0132 | 0x5a | | z | 122 | 0172 | 0x7a |
| (esc) | 27 | 0033 | 0x1b | | ; | 59 | 0073 | 0x3b | | [ | 91 | 0133 | 0x5b | | { | 123 | 0173 | 0x7b |
| (fs) | 28 | 0034 | 0x1c | | < | 60 | 0074 | 0x3c | | \ | 92 | 0134 | 0x5c | | \| | 124 | 0174 | 0x7c |
| (gs) | 29 | 0035 | 0x1d | | = | 61 | 0075 | 0x3d | | ] | 93 | 0135 | 0x5d | | } | 125 | 0175 | 0x7d |
| (rs) | 30 | 0036 | 0x1e | | > | 62 | 0076 | 0x3e | | ^ | 94 | 0136 | 0x5e | | ~ | 126 | 0176 | 0x7e |
| (us) | 31 | 0037 | 0x1f | | ? | 63 | 0077 | 0x3f | | _ | 95 | 0137 | 0x5f | | (del) | 127 | 0177 | 0x7f |

## APPENDIX B – END OF COURSE PROJECTS

## Practice Programming Projects

The best way to learn any programming language is to write programs.  This section provides ideas for projects for you to program.  See how many of these projects you can solve with what you have learned.  Read each one carefully and plan your approach to solve the problem.  These are all business / personal type projects from everyday problems.

Project 1      – Lumber
Project 2      – Shoe Store
Project 3      – China Project
Project 4      – Planet Weight
Project 5      – Dog Years
Project 6      – Coins Weight & Thickness
Project 7      – Mortgage Calculator
Project 8      – Change Maker
Project 9      – Currency Converter
Project 10     – Random Numbers (Lottery Picker) (Guess the Number) (Dice)

Explore different ways to write the various programs.  Enhance the programs, add functionality,  always try to make your program do more than the original design.  Try things and if you wreck your program, I hope you learn something like what NOT to do in a program.  This is software, you can't break anything.

# Project 1 -

## Lumber

The standard 2″ x 4″ board is not 2 inches by 4 inches. It may start that way but by the time the process is finished in producing the board it winds up smaller. Write a program that asks the user to select the lumber dimension and then displays the actual size in inches and metric. Use the following table for values:

| Nominal | Actual | Metric |
|---------|--------|--------|
| 1″ x 2″ | 3/4″ x 1-1/2″ | 19 x 38 mm |
| 1″ x 3″ | 3/4″ x 2-1/2″ | 19 x 64 mm |
| 1″ x 4″ | 3/4″ x 3-1/2″ | 19 x 89 mm |
| 1″ x 5″ | 3/4″ x 4-1/2″ | 19 x 114 mm |
| 1″ x 6″ | 3/4″ x 5-1/2″ | 19 x 140 mm |
| 1″ x 7″ | 3/4″ x 6-1/4″ | 19 x 159 mm |
| 1″ x 8″ | 3/4″ x 7-1/4″ | 19 x 184 mm |
| 1″ x 10″ | 3/4″ x 9-1/4″ | 19 x 235 mm |
| 1″ x 12″ | 3/4″ x 11-1/4″ | 19 x 286 mm |
| 2″ x 4″ | 1-1/2″ x 3-1/2″ | 38 x 89 mm |
| 2″ x 6″ | 1-1/2″ x 5-1/2″ | 38 x 140 mm |
| 2″ x 8″ | 1-1/2″ x 7-1/4″ | 38 x 184 mm |
| 2″ x 10″ | 1-1/2″ x 9-1/4″ | 38 x 235 mm |
| 2″ x 12″ | 1-1/2″ x 11-1/4″ | 38 x 286 mm |
| 3″ x 6″ | 2-1/2″ x 5-1/2″ | 64 x 140 mm |
| 4″ x 4″ | 3-1/2″ x 3-1/2″ | 89 x 89 mm |
| 4″ x 6″ | 3-1/2″ x 5-1/2″ | 89 x 140 mm |

## Project 2 –

### Shoe Store

A shoe store has asked you to provide a program for their store that allows a salesperson to find the price of various sneakers. The store carries four brands of sneakers and each brand has four different types of sneakers: Basketball; Fitness; Running; and Walking.

Create a simple, easy to use interface for a salesperson to obtain prices for various items carried by the store. The requirements for the program are as follows:

1. Allow the user to select a brand. Only one brand selected at a time.
2. Then the user will select the type of sneaker.
3. Allow the user to enter a quantity.
4. The user is then prompted to select either Adult or Children's sneakers.
5. The price is calculated using the price lists show below. The price list represents the store's cost for the sneakers, the user should see a price 30% higher than the price shown in the price list.
6. The form should show a date and time.

**Adult Price List**

|            | Adidas | Converse | Nike  | Reebok |
|------------|--------|----------|-------|--------|
| Basketball | $80    | $70      | $125  | $118   |
| Fitness    | $50    | $45      | $88   | $92    |
| Running    | $90    | $88      | $105  | $111   |
| Walking    | $80    | $71      | $79   | $89    |

**Children's Price List**

|            | Adidas | Converse | Nike  | Reebok |
|------------|--------|----------|-------|--------|
| Basketball | $60    | $65      | $117  | $106   |
| Fitness    | $35    | $38      | $104  | $100   |
| Running    | $55    | $62      | $109  | $110   |
| Walking    | $40    | $45      | $80   | $95    |

206

# Project 3 -

## China Project

A local fine china store has contracted you to write a program that will allow users to enter the Brand and the quantity of an item and receive a price quote. The interface should be attractive and easy to use for the user.

Basic system requirements are as follows:
1. Allow the user to choose among the 5 brands of china: Mikasa, Noritake, Farberware, Royal Daulton, and their house brand Ironstone.
2. Each brand can have 5 component pieces; Bowl, Butter Plate, Cup, Plate, Saucer. The user may order 1 or more of the component pieces.
3. The user can choose the number of place settings (all 5 pieces) that they wish, but they can only order quantities of 1, 2, 4, 6, or 12.
4. When the user chooses a brand, the component pieces, and the number of place settings, the price of the selected items should be displayed.
5. If the user forgets to select a brand, a number of place sittings or at least one component piece, then an error message should be displayed and the cursor positioned to reenter the missing information.
6. After verifying that the user has provided the application with all needed information, a calculated price should be displayed.

### China Price Matrix

| Brand | Piece | List Price | Brand | Piece | List Price |
|-------|-------|-----------|-------|-------|-----------|
| Mikasa | Bowl | $12 | Royal Daulton | Bowl | $10 |
| | Side Plate | $4 | | Side Plate | $8 |
| | Cup | $6 | | Cup | $5 |
| | Plate | $18 | | Plate | $6 |
| | Saucer | $4 | | Saucer | $3 |
| | | | | | |
| Noritake | Bowl | $6 | Ironstone | Bowl | $1 |
| | Side Plate | $2 | | Side Plate | $2 |
| | Cup | $3 | | Cup | $3 |
| | Plate | $9 | | Plate | $4 |

| Brand | Piece | List Price | | Brand | Piece | List Price |
|---|---|---|---|---|---|---|
| | Saucer | $2 | | | Saucer | $2 |
| | | | | | | |
| Farberware | Bowl | $5 | | | | |
| | Side Plate | $3 | | | | |
| | Cup | $4 | | | | |
| | Plate | $8 | | | | |
| | Saucer | $3 | | | | |

If you order a complete set (all 5 pieces) you must order in quantities of 1, 2, 4, 6, or 12. Complete sets of 4 or 6 receive a 5% discount, sets of 12 receive a discount of 10%.

You are to come up with your original design with emphasis on visually attractive and user friendly.

# Project 4 –

## Planet Weight

The effects of gravity on various planets will affect your weight. Using Earth weight as our baseline for our weight, create a program that will ask for the users weight on earth and then determine the weight value for each of the other planets.

| Planet | Multiply By |
|---|---|
| Mercury | 0.37 |
| Venus | 0.88 |
| Mars | 0.38 |
| Jupiter | 2.64 |
| Saturn | 1.20 |
| Neptune | 1.12 |
| Uranus | 1.15 |
| Pluto | 0.04 |

Design a program that allows the user to select a planet, enter the weight and the program produces the calculated weight on the planet selected.

Some variations
- Enter weight and display the calculation on the form.
- Enter weight and display the calculation in a MessageBox
- Enter weignt and display on the form for all planets.
- Get additional facts about each planet and display along with the weight.
- Planet selections using radio buttons, check boxes, drop down list, etc.

## Project 5 -

### Dog Years Converter

This program will calculate the number of months alive, given the years and the months old.  The user enters the age in years and months and the program calculates and displays the number of months alive.  Then calculates the age in dog years and displays that information also.


Some Variations:
- Use other animal life calculations.
- When multiple animals calculated, use radio buttons, check boxes, drop down lists, etc.
- Develop conversion programs for other topics
  - metric
  - distance
  - measurements

# Project 6 -

## Coins - Weight

You have saved coins in a big jar. Now it is time to cash in. Counting all those coin will be a big pain but you want to have some idea how much you have saved before going to the bank. You researched the weight of coins and found the following table on the internet.

| Denomination | Weight | Thickness |
|:---:|:---|:---|
| $0.01 | 2.500 grams | 1.52 millimeters |
| $0.05 | 5.000 grams | 1.95 millimeters |
| $0.10 | 2.268 grams | 1.35 millimeters |
| $0.25 | 5.670 grams | 1.75 millimeters |
| $0.50 | 11.340 grams | 2.15 millimeters |
| $1.00 | 8.1 grams | 2.00 millimeters |

You decide to sort your coins by denomination and then weigh the pennies, nickels, dimes, quarters, half-dollars, and dollars and use their weight and the above table to calculate the approximate value of the coins.

Write a program that asks the user for the denomination, the total weight of the coins of that denomination, and the program calculates how many coins and their approximate value. The program displays the value of the coins and asks for the next denomination. When the user quits the program, a table is displayed with the denomination, the number of coins, and the value. The program will also display the total value of all the coins.
NOTE: Multiply Ounces by 28 to get Grams.


## Coins – Stacks

You have saved coins in a big jar. Now it is time to cash in. Counting all those coin will be a big pain but you want to have some idea how much you have saved before going to the bank. You researched the thickness of coins and found the following table on the internet.

| Denomination | Weight | Thickness |
|:---:|:---|:---|
| $0.01 | 2.500 grams | 1.52 millimeters |
| $0.05 | 5.000 grams | 1.95 millimeters |
| $0.10 | 2.268 grams | 1.35 millimeters |
| $0.25 | 5.670 grams | 1.75 millimeters |
| $0.50 | 11.340 grams | 2.15 millimeters |
| $1.00 | 8.1 grams | 2.00 millimeters |

You decide to sort your coins by denomination and then measure the stacks of the pennies, nickels, dimes, quarters, half-dollars, and dollars and use their thickness and the above table to calculate the approximate value of the coins.

Write a program that asks the user for the denomination, the height of the stack of the coins of that denomination, and the program calculates how many coins and their approximate value. The program displays the value of the coins and asks for the next denomination. When the user quits the program, a table is displayed with the denomination, the number of coins, and the value. The program will also display the total value of all the coins.
NOTE: Divide Inches by 0.039370 to get Millimeters.

# Project 7 -

## Mortgage Calculator

Write a program to calculate the Monthly Payment for a mortgage using the following information:

       Principal Amount
       Interest Rate
       Term (length of loan 30 years, 20 years, 10 years)

Use the Formula:
Monthly Payment = Principal * MonthInt / (1-(1/(1+MonthInt)) ^ (Years * 12))

MonthInt = Interest Rate / 12

The user enters the information into a form. Enter the Principal Amount in Dollars and Cents, the Interest Rate as a decimal (EXAMPLE: 3.95% entered as .0395) and the term which can be 30 years, 20 years or 10 years. The program should validate the data in all three entries.

## Project 8 -

**Change Maker**

Develop a program that allows the user to enter a sale amount between $0.01 and $99.99. Then ask for a payment amount between $0.01 and $100.00. Then ask the user for the change due. The program should calculate the change due and if the user entered the correct amount, display the users estimate, the actual amount and if they match print "CORRECT!". If the amounts do not match print the message to a messagebox "TRY AGAIN!".

Then ask the user how many of each denomination should be returned in change. Denominations of $50; $20; $10; $5; $1; $0.50; $0.25; $0.10; $0.05; and $0.01 may be used. The program should calculate the optimum denominations to make the change and compare to what the user selected. If a match, Congratulations, if not a match, a messagebox asking the user to „TRY AGAIN!"

## Project 9 -

Currency Converter

Write a program that asks for a whole dollar amount from the user and select the foreign currency from a list. Then does a currency conversion from US Dollars entered to the currency selected. Use the following table for conversion factors.

| Currency | Conversion Factor |
|---|---|
| Euro | 0.730 |
| English Pound | 0.595 |
| Japanese Yen | 101.545 |
| Russian Ruble | 34.745 |
| Mexican Peso | 12.893 |
| Canadian Dollar | 1.086 |
| Korean Won | 1,024.100 |
| Norwegian Krone | 5.934 |

Some variations to this program are:
1. Put the table in an array.
2. Put the table in a file.
3. Convert from the foreign currency to US Dollars.
4. Select a from currency and a to currency and convert.
5. Get additional conversion factors and include more currencies.

## Project 10 -

Random Numbers (Lottery Picker) (Guess the Number) (Dice)

Project A – Simple Dice Game

In the text there is an illustration of a program that rolls two dice, and totals the two amounts. Use this as a basis for a program for two players. Players alternate turns and the sum of each roll is added to a counter. The first one to reach 100 wins the game.

Project B – Guess the Number

In this project the computer selects a random number between 1 and 100. The user is then prompted to guess the number. If the guess is too low the program should respond "LOW" and allow another guess. If the guess is too high the program should respond "HIGH" and allows another guess. If the user guesses the number print out a message of success and the program ends.

Project C – Lottery Picker

Lottery games like Powerball and Mega Millions are played by millions of people. Some have their magic numbers, others just let the computer pick their numbers. Write a program for Powerball or Mega Millions, using their number rules. The program should allow the user to pick numbers for one to twenty tickets.